Endorsements

Carol Giles' *Calming the Chaos: How to Live Beautifully in a Broken World* is the product of a deep passion on her part. She has long had a strong compassion for disciples who are moving from a light, culturally motivated commitment to their faith to a more fully committed relationship with God. I most appreciate the many instances where she shares her own steps and missteps in that journey. I recommend the book especially for those who want to share a pilgrimage towards living more closely to the heart of the Christian life.

— Jim Coleman, D. Min., Former pastor, and contributor to the Life Application Bible

Calming the Chaos by Carol Giles is an amazing book written by an amazing woman who deeply loves an amazing God. I highly recommend it for anyone who feels satisfied or bored with the Christian faith. Her penetrating insights won't leave you the same!

— Michael J. Klassen, Former pastor, best-selling ghostwriter, author, and publisher

Testimonial, relevant for our Age, evangelistic, globally-thoughtful, theological informative, practical, and healing – Carol Giles writes a book for our generation.

– Shane Calvillo, M.Div, Associate Pastor of Grace Community Church.

Calming the Chaos addresses critical life issues in a provocative yet accessible manner. Regardless of whether you agree with the author's premise or her conclusions, her arguments for the existence and intervention of a loving God in the world, and the impact His presence should have on our lives will give serious readers much to think about.

– Doyle Baker, Assistant District Attorney, Colorado Springs, El Paso County, Colorado

This refreshing book calls us to awaken in a living, breathing relationship with our Creator, fully expressed in Jesus of Nazareth. Our haphazard, non-intentional expressions of faith will not suffice. Either Christianity stands on its own merits as the answer to the fallen condition we find ourselves in or it does not. Come experience, in this cleverly written memoir along with prose, the story of

Carol, and indeed, the story of us all: our broken state before a holy God, who himself condescends in Jesus to meet our greatest need and reconciles us to a good and faithful Father. In the end, this book speaks to the story of God, the author of our lives and salvation. We are but a piece in His drama of redemption. For reasons beyond us, God has chosen the foolish things of this world (us) to shame the wise (and dare even bring hope to them). Carol weaves beautifully through her own story and brings to bear the very Word of God, which is the final arbiter of truth – how are we to live and think as believers in this world until its final culmination? One would do well to head the words herein and wrestle through their practical implications. Perhaps, it too could change your life.

– Mike Burch, MA, Denver Seminary

CALMING THE CHAOS:

How to Live Beautifully in a Broken World

Carol Flohr Giles

CALMING
THE CHAOS

Unless otherwise noted, Scripture quotations are taken from the HOLY BIBLE: NEW INTERNATIONAL VERSION®. © 1973, 1978, 1984 by International Bible Society. Used by permission of Zondervan Publishing House. All rights reserved.

Scriptures marked MSG are from *The Message* by Eugene H. Peterson. © 1993, 1994, 1995, 1996, 2000. Used by permission of NavPress Publishing Group. All rights reserved.

Scriptures marked TLB are from *The Living Bible*. © 1971. Used by permission of Tyndale House Publishers, Inc., Wheaton, Illinois 60189. All rights reserved.

Scriptures marked ESV are from THE ENGLISH STANDARD VERSION. © 2001 by Crossway Bibles, a division of Good News Publishers.

Scriptures marked NASB are from the New American Standard Bible® (NASB), Copyright © 1960, 1962, 1963, 1968, 1971, 1972, 1973, 1975, 1977, 1995 by The Lockman Foundation Used by permission. www.Lockman.org.

Library of Congress Cataloging-in-Publication Data

Names: Giles, Carol Flohr. author.
Title: Calming the Chaos: How to Live Beautifully in a Broken World/Carol Flohr Giles
Description: Littleton, CO: Clay Pot Publishing

Subjects: World—Culture—Religion—Creation—Worldview—Christian Living

Print: 978-1-947360-06-8
eBook: 978-1-947360-07-5

Printed in the United States of America

Cover design by Debbie Lewis

Author photograph by Robert Campbell Photography

Prepared and packaged by Illumify Media Group
IllumifyMedia.com
"We Make Your Writing Shine"

Contents

Introduction

To be loved but not known is comforting but superficial. To be known and not loved is our greatest fear. But to be fully known and truly loved is, well, a lot like being loved by God. It is what we need more than anything. It liberates us from pretense, humbles us out of our self-righteousness, and fortifies us for any difficulty life can throw at us.

– Tim Keller

His name was Aylan. He was 3 years old, from war-torn Syria. His final journey was supposed to end in sanctuary in Europe; instead it claimed his life and highlighted the plight of desperate people caught in the gravest refugee crisis since World War II.

– The Wall Street Journal

Police say a mother set her newborn baby on fire in the middle of a road in Pemberton Township, N.J., late Friday.

– USA Today

Four women were held captive in a Denver garage last week where they were pistol-whipped, sexually assaulted and threatened with drug overdoses.

– The Denver Post

Turkey vowed on Monday to "completely cleanse" Islamic State militants from its border region after a suicide bomber suspected of links to the group killed 54 people, including 22 children, at a Kurdish wedding.

– World News

Sickened by these events, we wring our hands, we attend vigils, we light candles, but nothing seems to change. The daily tragedies continue and we go on with our lives, and wonder how and when the brokenness in our world will stop. "What is wrong with these people?" we ask ourselves.

Recently, a jet-black, four-wheel drive truck pulled up next to me at a stoplight. The truck was so high from the ground, I would have needed a ladder to get in. Sitting side by side, waiting for the light to change, I noticed something written on the driver's side fender in bright red letters: "Kill em' All". The truck pulled away, and I saw a moose head trailer hitch cover. My thoughts wandered aimlessly:

Who does he want to kill? Maybe he's a hunter. He could be against illegal immigrants or Muslims. Maybe he's a racist, a redneck, or a Special Forces Marine just home from battle. What is wrong with this person?

I asked my Christian counselor the same question about my former husband who whipped my 5-year-old son across the face with his belt, and she replied, "He was a sociopath."

A sociopath shows disregard for others, lacks remorse, is manipulative, egocentric, and lies to get what they want. Yet to know that *those people* might be sociopaths doesn't help us much, does it? We want to blame something or someone.

Society condemns radicalized jihadists, black activists, mentally unstable youths, white supremacists, overzealous law enforcement officers, gang members, druggies, or people acting out their childhood experiences. "How could God allow such things to happen?" we ask. God is not to blame. The blame is sin, my sin, your sin, all the sin in the world.

The chaos in the world surrounds us with unimaginable acts of terror and

Time Out

Why should we blame the brokenness of the world on sin? God gave us the ability to make our own decisions: good, bad, right, or wrong. That may be true, but the bad decisions made by murderers are sin. Furthermore, the apostle, Paul tells us, "For all have sinned and fall short of the glory of God" (Rom. 3:23).

we need comfort. We need genuine love, connections with people who care for us, and a stable dimension in our lives that never changes. This book will be your chaperon and companion on your pilgrimage through its pages where you will learn, as I did, that a relationship with the living God is the only way to live beautifully in the brokenness of this world.

It wasn't always that way for me, so let me share my story. Back when I thought I wasn't a sinner, but instead a good person trying to do the right things, a pastor asked all the "sinners" in the congregation to stand. I stayed seated. But I noticed that the very "best" people stood up.

For many of my adult years, I lived as though God made little difference to me. My Christian existence focused on tradition, earthly and temporal things, and material gain, instead of faith. God protected and loved me, even though I was never there for him. I loved myself, not God. He caused the sun to rise, the moon to shine, and the stars to come out at night. That seemed sufficient to me. And even though I hadn't given God a second thought, I expected him to rescue me whenever I was hit with a curve ball in life, such as the crash of our business computer. I prayed, "God, why are you doing this to me?" I felt sorry for myself and I complained.

Furthermore, I was never satisfied. Often my experiences with overwhelming sadness as a child and teenager reappeared. Contrary and compulsive, my few friends didn't understand my quirkiness, but they tolerated it. Unable to understand my actions, I lived with unresolved anger and bitterness. I wondered, "What's wrong with me? Why can't I be happy like everyone else?"

By the time I was twenty-four years old, I found myself single. I had been married twice, having birthed three children with my first husband and one with my second. I didn't plan to marry again, but then I met my third husband, who adopted my four children, and we've been married for forty-nine years. We were not biblical Christians when we married, but when my Uncle Russ and Aunt Izzy moved near us, we witnessed two people who were fully committed to their faith in God for the first time in our lives.

Russ, Izzy, and their two children, lived fifteen minutes away. Our two families became close, because although Russ was my uncle, two of my children were close in age to theirs. We ate meals together, hiked together, prayed together, and attended church together. I wanted what Russ and Izzy had; I turned my life over to Jesus Christ quietly and alone.

My low-key conversion experience to Christianity started me on a difficult, mind- bending road. My feelings of unworthiness over my past caused shame, and I started lying. I pretended that my marriage was my first and that I had graduated from high school. Although I had converted to Christianity, I didn't feel like a true believer. I looked forward to a new life; I called myself a Christian and attended church every Sunday. Still, I lived complacent and unaware, habitually daydreaming about elusive contentment, always seeking, never finding. Years passed.

As I thought about my history with God, I grudgingly remembered growing up and trying to conform to the behavioral patterns of my parents. Unable to imagine that I was part of something greater than myself, I believed everything about me was connected to them, even though our relationship was distant. My family's limited dinner conversations focused on my dad's work.

When my sister and I were bold enough to ask questions, the yes or no answers stopped the conversation. My father focused on his business, and my mother focused on my father. My sister, almost five years older than me, and I shared little in common due to our age difference, so we focused on ourselves. Our family included God only on Sunday mornings and the pastor preached with a dramatic flair, which pleased my parents.

"I thought the pulpit was going to crack when he slammed his fist down, didn't you?" Mom asked Dad one day on our way home from church. Soon they became good friends with the pastor and his wife. Later, after joining the church choir, my parents discussed the music and sermons, and always talked about how it might have affected the congregation. Discussions about a transcendent and personal God did not exist. "Religion is personal," Mom said. Later, as I yearned for more inside, I loathed myself on the outside.

My heart thirsted for fresh knowledge and I wanted to live authentically. I grappled with unworthiness and I wanted to know who I was, why I lived, and what God had planned for my life. "Will there ever be a time when I please God enough for him to make plans for me?" I asked myself.

There were no answers to my question. Forcing myself into a corner, I avoided conversation with people in church because of my lies. I avoided social events with my friends from high school because I feared they would think I was a Jesus freak. I assumed my social life should be with Christians. My self-imposed island was so small that there was nowhere to turn. I stood in the center and looked out, but there wasn't one safe place to keep myself afloat. I felt parched from lack of intimacy with God.

In my early fifties, I picked up the Life Application Bible my husband gave me. It had sat unopened for months. Reading and studying the Bible became a daily ritual. Still, my quiet times took their toll because I learned what an authentic Christian should be. I thought I was an authentic Christian, but my studies told a different story.

It was apparent that I needed to kill false spirituality, tradition, and apathy to make room for a personal relationship with God. The lives of biblical people such as, Abraham, Moses, Isaiah, David, and Paul, brought me comfort and clarity, because they were fallen human beings, just like me. Nevertheless, I needed to confront my sin just as they did.

But I was terrified. To reject family sin patterns like materialism, perfectionism, bad language, and daily alcohol consumption made me fearful of losing close friends and family members who listened, but politely changed the subject when they heard me talk about God.

There I stood, on the brink of reality, and not liking it very much.

Societal boxes hadn't worked in the past, so I contemplated what would work for me now in order to gain a comprehensive view of reality. As a first-time faith explorer, I tried to research my identity in the world. The facts that I believed in God and knew that God had created me prompted deliberate and decisive action.

I ran into new discoveries about myself while writing my memoir, *Call of the Potter*, which brought me understanding about my past. After spending time reading the Bible, the hardships of my life became blessings. I discovered that God had watched out for me, and I concluded that while he waited patiently for me, he also sheltered me. He lavished me with grace. He loved me. He forgave me. Most importantly, he revealed himself to me.

Paradoxically, I still felt destitute, deprived, and disconnected in my soul. It occurred to me that I was capable of any of the crimes headlined in the *Wall Street Journal, USA Today, The Denver Post*, or *World News*.

As my own worst enemy, I started to ask myself questions. "What to do? How to do it?" Became my mantras, whirling through my head like a flock of vultures, ready to pick at and devour every thought, like the carcass of a dead animal. Then a plan for realignment started developing in my mind, to see myself in a new way, as a person created by God, yet a sinner. The blueprint lay before me, and although the specifications loomed as real life obstacles, just having a plan gave me courage.

My eyes saw and my ears opened wide to the cosmic talent and artistry of God when I read and studied Psalm 139:13–16:

> *For you created my inmost being; you knit me together in my mother's womb. I praise you because I am fearfully and wonderfully made; your works are wonderful, I know that full well. My frame was not hidden from you when I was made in the secret place, when I was woven together in the depths of the earth. Your eyes saw my unformed body; all the days ordained for me were written in your book before one of them came to be.*

God had beckoned me. Sequestered and set apart, I found myself resting in the arms of Jesus. There would be no turning back. Smitten, I gave myself over to God. He had made me for specific purposes—he made me capable, and he had plans for me. My admissions of unfaithfulness humbled me, while an obscure frame of reference came into view. Building my new life on the rock-solid foundation of God's Word, I brought rational thought, based on objective truth, into the folds of my mind.

So why would I want to bare my soul, and write about my lack of spiritual integrity, inattention to my thoughts and actions, my foolish mistakes, and unkindness to others? Because, my heart weeps for family members, friends, and other people in the world who don't know Jesus. It's not enough to know about Jesus. When we really know him, our lives take a 180 degree turn. We find ourselves on the most amazing journey that helps us deal with brokenness and teaches us how to live beautifully.

To see the world realistically is hard. On the other hand, trying to blot out the immorality, violence, and lack of grace shown to one another, doesn't work for me. It's like reading a bad book with a bad ending. The pages turn, one after another, without any calming of the chaos. The only solution is that the world needs God.

Now, I know some of you are thinking, "That's a bunch of bull. And it's that kind of broad statement that turns me off about Christianity." I get it. Still, through my relationship with God, he changed me from a confrontational, never satisfied, sad person into a person who can risk telling her story, warts and all, to help others find the peace I have.

I spent part of my life without God, which means I relate to unresolved anger, low self- esteem, and unhappiness. And because I recognize those feelings and acknowledge them, I'm a different person today. However, I know that I am just as capable of vile and treacherous acts as anybody else, except that God's grace surrounds me with love and gives me strength.

This book is a work of my heart. Perhaps, it will encourage people whose faith falters in the midst of a decaying world. Maybe it will bring faith to the forefront of someone's life who has no faith. If one person grasps the eternal beauty of the gospel message and resists the behavioral patterns of the world, then that person will tell others and so on. Today we call it "paying it forward."

With fresh discoveries to share, I want to be courageous and honest by telling the truth: a relationship with Jesus Christ is the only way we can make sense of the world and all its failures. This confuses many people. Some are reluctant to give their lives to Jesus and live under his authority. Others think they will have to change themselves or do things they don't want to. And there are those who might say, "Well it can't be as easy as that." These misgivings are understandable. But, it is as easy as that. And the changes? God initiates the changes. And then we respond naturally and gradually to his love, grace, mercy, and guidance.

I don't know all the answers, but my goal for this book is to look at universal concepts we all can identify with, that may provide some of you with the answers you're looking for. These concepts include:

Creation

Creation, the beginning of all things, is where we learn that God made each one of us for specific purposes and that he made us good. We are not junk. When we think of God as our heavenly Father and compare him to our earthly father, it helps us understand God in ways we would never imagine.

Cultures

Cultures are different pockets of societies and their belief systems that either contribute to the grace, decency, and love shown to others or cause degradation of others through the misuse of power, greed, depravity, and self-indulgence. Since we are not always aware of how cultural trends of indifference toward biblical faith trickle down to society, we fall prey to ideologies that are abrasive to our collective conscience.

False Identities

False identities are labels that we unknowingly assign to those who are different from us will create havoc in our relationships. Too often, we listen to and believe errant media observations about certain people without asking them what they believe and why.

Political Pressure

Political pressure occurs when our view is different from those in our surrounding culture; this pressure removes the freedom to verbalize how and why we believe as we do. The compulsion to pursue "correctness," has transformed us into a nation of tolerance at the expense of truth.

Healthy Self-awareness

Healthy self-awareness, a lost concept of who we are and what we think, has become self- indulgence. Society needs to re-discover why we think as we do and how it influences our actions. The lack of focus on how our character, motivations, emotions, and desires guide our thoughts and actions has turned us into an "it's all about me" culture.

Biblical Precepts

Biblical precepts encompass whether we believe what the Bible says or not. These precepts offer common sense solutions to our lives, while giving pertinent and realistic ways to view the world's problems, and how to live beautifully in spite of them.

Worldview Thinking

Worldview thinking is the common denominator to our lives; it informs and instructs our thoughts and actions. It shows us how our reactions to the world define our core beliefs. Our worldview creates a value system from which we make decisions and/or make boundaries for ourselves. And it helps us make sense of the world as it is, and what it might become.

As we consider each of these universal concepts throughout the book, here are some questions to consider:

How do these universal concepts inform our faith?

Do they breed confidence or hatch criticism?

What do our souls thirst for within the context of the universe?

Is it too late for us? Is there no hope for America? Is there no hope for the world?

At the end of every chapter, you'll find a list of questions that pertain to the chapter content. Not intended to be intrusive, they are for your introspection, perhaps to record in a journal, encourage you, or refresh your memory. Please read them and think about them. I pray that your reflections will bring you renewed wholeness in your mind, body, and spirit.

PART I

THE WORLD
IN WHICH WE LIVE

I am good, but not an angel
I do sin, but I am not the devil
I am just a small girl in a big world
trying to find someone to love

– Marilyn Monroe

CHAPTER ONE

Secular Society

Some people believe the alternative to bad religion is secularism, but that's wrong . . . The answer to bad religion is better religion--prophetic rather than partisan, broad and deep instead of narrow, and based on values as opposed to ideology.

– Jim Wallis

"I'M NOT GOING to church," the young man said as he sat at the kitchen bar. His dark eyes were piercing and his angular jaw was set.

"What do you mean you're not going to church?" his mom, Linda, asked.

"Exactly what I said, 'I'm not going to church.'"

"Why Trevor? You loved youth group and we've always gone to church as a family."

"Mom, I joined the Secular Student Alliance at school."

"What in the world is that?" Linda asked.

"It's a place where I can feel comfortable without being bombarded by religion, rituals, and rules. Our organization gives non-theists an environment that's free from bigotry, dogmatism, and superstition."

"Non-theists? Does that mean you don't believe in God anymore? Trevor, I'm begging you. Please go to church with me," Linda said, fighting back tears.

Trevor stood up, knocked the bar stool over and shouted, "Mom! I'm not into religion anymore," as he stormed out of the kitchen.

Separation of Church and State is not the Same as Secularism

Secularists don't recognize a transcendent being. And while they insist on leaving God out of government, education, and public parts of society, separation of church

> **Time Out**
>
> What does "separation of church and state" really mean? We are familiar with the phrase because it is part of the First Amendment in the U.S. Constitution. It allows citizens the freedom to practice the religion of their choice and prevents the government from officially recognizing or favoring any specific religion. Secularism, on the other hand, believes that religion should not play a role in government, education, or be visible in other public parts of society. The difference is that the First Amendment allows for practice of religion—all religion—publicly, whereas secularism does not.

and state is not the same as secularism—not when the government prints "In God We Trust" on our money.

Most politicians end their speeches with the words, "God Bless You" while others add "and God Bless America." Historically, Americans look at God as a supreme being with whom we have a "special relationship." And most Americans believe God will continue to favor us.

According to the Secular Coalition for America, eighteen different secularist organizations exist in the United States who have the power to change society/ culture through their members' power at the ballot box These bright, rational, skeptics identify themselves as agnostics, atheists, freethinkers, humanists, non-theists, and naturalists, according to the Center for Inquiry.

Is That All There Is?

For many, atheism or agnosticism isn't enough, so their preference is the secular humanism movement. Some Secular Humanists ask the question, "Is that all there is?" They also offer solutions to people who reject God. According to the Council for Secular Humanism, they believe it's liberating to recognize that supernatural beings are human creations. They regard people as random, unintended, and responsible for themselves.

As offensive as this statement of rejection must be to God, the oft-repeated phrase, "Is That All There Is?" from Peggy Lee's classic song presents us with an opportunity to explore society and ourselves. If we ignore this call to action, we can't help but fall into the trap of defining humanity as accidental beings: aimless, purposeless, without spirit, and ignorant to the matchless wonders of creation.

The Ethical Culture movement doesn't consider itself a religion. However, some members choose to believe in a deity and categorize their religion as one that adheres to beliefs or institutions that bind human behaviors and emotions to something other than self. This "binding … to something other than self" shows that those who believe in a deity are searching for a steady relationship with someone or something greater than they are. They want relief and comfort from the brokenness of the world just like you and me.

By denying spiritual hunger, the secularist culture leaves followers to yearn for meaning, hope, forgiveness, intimacy, and to ask cosmic questions for which there are no answers. Therein lies their problem. They simply cannot believe in something that doesn't answer their questions or they can't touch and see.

Forced to choose between religion and science, secularists turn to science, while Christians turn to religion. Each view has its critics because each requires a certain level of faith. Even science isn't absolute. Theories that have stood for hundreds of years are often disproven as we learn more about the universe. For example, although some Christians deny the "big bang" theory, in the last part of the twentieth century, certain religious and scientific communities have concluded that intelligent design (God) was instrumental in the causation of the big bang. The thought here is that without intelligent design, the universe would have disintegrated along with any potential for life after the bang.

We don't have all the facts concerning creation, and even if we did, our understanding would be insufficient, diverse, and provocative to those who disagree. Bang or not, God intelligently designed our universe, in ways that are incomprehensible to the human mind. In Hebrews we read, "By faith we understand that the universe was formed at God's command, so that what is seen was not made out of what was visible" (Hebrews 11:3). God doesn't have to prove anything to us. And he doesn't need our help to reveal himself in mysterious ways.

My friend, Judy, was an atheist during her first years of college. Due to a serious illness, she withdrew from school for a semester. Judy didn't understand why this happened to her. But when she returned to school, she met up with the student who had moved into her dorm room while she was away.

"I cannot thank you enough for your dorm room while you were away," the student said.

"What do you mean?" Judy asked.

"Well, if your room hadn't been vacant for that particular semester, I wouldn't have moved into it, and I wouldn't have met the man I plan to marry after I finish school."

"Oh, okay. That's great."

Forced to live in a "party" dorm, surrounded by noise and loud music, Judy hoped to get a room in her old dorm. While Judy suffered, the other student enjoyed the benefits of a quiet room. As a kind of apology, the future bride, who was a Christian, quoted Scripture to Judy:

And we know that in all things God works for the good of those who love him, who have been called according to his purpose (Rom. 8:28).

She said that those words "niggled" at her for a long time. Wondering how she might look at the situation differently, she concluded that the other student and her fiancé had something in their lives that she wanted. Unable to figure out what that something was, Judy felt compelled to think about it. For the first time in her life, Judy thought about the atheistic idea that no transcendent being exists, began to question atheism, and ultimately experienced a divine revelation. Confident that her illness benefited the future bride, she believed that a cosmic being had caused this unexplainable situation to come about. Judy is now a committed Christian.

Many Uninformed and Vulnerable Christians Believe in Secularist Ideas

Secularism is a belief system, not a religion, and although we may be inclined to leave God out of secular beliefs, we might want to admit to the reality that many uninformed and vulnerable Christians believe in secularist ideas. For example, many Christians unintentionally exclude original sin (everyone is born a sinner) from their faith, because they choose to believe in the basic goodness of people. I agree that is a happier, more enjoyable way to look at the world, but it doesn't explain the depravity in the world.

Happiness and enjoyment are emotional states framed by circumstances. For example, when we are happily married, we are ecstatic, but the moment we learn that our spouse is having an affair with our best friend, we are devastated. To amplify the point I'm making, if a parent hasn't experienced the senseless murder of their child, they can certainly view people as basically good. On the other hand, the parent placing a single rose on top of a small coffin sees the depravity of people for the rest of their life.

Further, Secularists dismiss the spirit world, reject miracles, and ignore the fact that all good things come from God. Still, their question of why God allows bad things to happen is understandable. However, when people who rely on their faith suffer loss and tragedy, instead of blaming God, they hunker down and lean into their faith to see them through.

Secularists, unaware of the Christian belief that talents and achievements are from God, believe they are responsible for all the good in their lives. The disparity between these two perceptions creates enormous gaps in how humanity acts and reacts to the events happening around them, whether directly or not. If we believe we are responsible for our talent as a ballerina, does that mean we are the culprits when we can no longer perform, because we lost our leg in a freak accident? What then? Regrettably, it's been my experience that some who don't value God's gifts, blame God when things go awry. Isn't this a case of displaced blame? If we don't believe in God, then why would we blame God during our calamities? Please don't misunderstand. Some Christians do the same thing.

It's no secret that there are fewer religious people in the twenty-first century. The Huffington Post notes, "Millennials are significantly less religious than previous generations of young Americans." Still, some consider themselves religious, but they regard their religion as personal and private, as if it were beside the point and unnecessary. Aloof and unaffected by their faith, biblical thinking isn't part of who they are. Their faith has no lasting effect on how they live. Instead, their workplaces, classrooms, book clubs, and social connections influence them greatly. Some call this Secular Christianity. People believe they are Christians, but their religion is one of convenience. In other words, they may tell their friend they'll help them move, but when the day arrives, something more enjoyable has popped up and they don't follow through with what their commitment. Also, they might apply dual concepts to their lives, by putting spiritual things in the sacred category and worldly things in the secular category. The Bible tells a different story; we can't have it both ways.

> *Stop loving this evil world and all that it offers you, for when you love these things you show that you do not really love God; for all these worldly things, these evil desires—the craze for sex, the ambition to buy everything that appeals to you, and the pride that comes from wealth and importance—these are not from God. They are from this evil world itself. And this world is fading away, and these evil, forbidden things will go with it, but whoever keeps doing the will of God will live forever* (1 John 2:15–17, TLB).

Time Out

If I follow God, does that mean I can't have nice things? This is a question many people, including Christians, ask; of course, you can have nice things. Following God isn't a vow of poverty for most of us. Feel free to enjoy nice things, but recognize they are only temporary (as is our enjoyment of them) and they won't feed your soul. God is not opposed to our achieving material wealth. We just can't do so by taking advantage of others or through unethical ways. We also shouldn't live beyond our means or avoid regular tithing. You may find your greatest satisfaction is not achieving material wealth for its own sake, but in the good you can do by supporting worthy causes.

By either denying, forgetting, or being ignorant of what the Bible says, the Secular Christian assumes that God will never triumph over evil, that God's will won't prevail. It's as if they've thrown their hands up in the air, claiming, "It's of no use. There's nothing that can change this sick, sadistic, sleazy world."

Secular Christians who deny God's sovereignty but attend church regularly place God in the sacred compartment. On the way home, they shut down the sacred compartment, open the secular compartment, and live the rest of the week as if God doesn't exist. I can relate to Secular Christians, because for a long time after I accepted Christ, I attended church every Sunday, but that was the extent of my commitment.

Further, some people act as if their faith means nothing while living in a secular world. For example, they may look at the first or second date hook-up as normal, and shrug their shoulders. Watching a female television news anchor wear revealing clothing, they might choose to do the same in their workplace. Furthermore, the inclination to follow along with celebrities' values shows lack of thought, because the private persona of a celebrity may be different from what we see in public. My point is this: if living in a secular world doesn't cause some people of faith to re-evaluate their priorities, perhaps they're not being honest with themselves.

We Can't Disregard the Carnage and Catastrophic Events in the World

Spiritual hunger is real. We long for something greater than ourselves. We yearn to make a difference. We want significance in our small story as it pertains to the larger, cosmic drama of life. We crave meaning, worth, purpose, and genuine connections to others. And while some Secularists claim that life is meaningless and all morality is relative, they may not be aware of or want to admit these longings, they may think they determine their own purpose in life. Nevertheless, many admit to their desire for an everlasting purpose, to exist eternally, but outside the context of faith. In addition, while some people feel stable and immune to the depravity around us, if they believe in God, they can't disregard the carnage and catastrophic events in the world.

On the other hand, if they don't believe in the sovereignty of God, they may unknowingly disrupt the sense of security in their lives. Furthermore, children and teens, who hear and understand more than we think, are reluctant to talk about their concerns. They remain silent, often suffering from anxiety and fear.

And while trying to minimize our feelings of despair, we may plummet into the abyss of selfishness, greed, and distortion of the truth about ourselves. Uninformed, we become products of a culture that doesn't give a damn. We pattern ourselves after subjective ideologies without noticing. As an example, while living in South Korea, my husband and I experienced a receiving line tradition in which we Americans would greet the first Korean standing in an upright position, while the Korean bows at the waist. By the time we had reached the end of the line, we were unaware that we'd begun to greet each Korean with a bow at the waist.

We're living in a world that promotes freedom, individuality, and subjectivity. Recently, I read about a woman, Shelia who said her religion was an "ism" of herself. Do we really want this self-proclaimed philosophy to result in other isms, "Susanism," "Maryism," or "Johnism?" This woman's "ism" came from her personalized idea of how she wanted to live. By constructing her own boundaries, she could alter her moral code to fit the occasion, the place, or the people at any given time. At this point, her religion is merchandise, modified to meet her expectations like a piece of clothing. She might even choose to market it, by promoting her "style" of religion.

Broad skepticism, suspicion of reason, and sensitivity to political and economic power is partly responsible for certain church movements. Diverse groups of people who call themselves Christians are determined to communicate with today's world by reinventing God's will, twisting Christian beliefs, and, in essence, abandoning God. They focus on their Christianity as a tool to gain and manage political and economic power. And by mixing secularist ideologies with Christian truth, they drift into the dangerous zone of not truly understanding what they believe.

For example, in a conversation with a friend, I referred to Satan as the devil.

"You don't really believe in the devil, do you?" she asked.

"Of course I do," I replied.

In another conversation, I explained the foolishness of a New Age church in our area advertising its annual Easter Service.

"They don't really believe in Jesus, and since Easter celebrates the resurrection of Jesus, what's the point?" I asked.

"No, I think they believe in Jesus," she replied.

"They may believe there was a Jesus, but they certainly don't believe that Jesus is God," I said.

"Oh, I see what you mean. I hadn't thought about it that way."

My friend believes in God. She just wasn't aware of the difference between believing in Jesus and believing that Jesus is God. Some Secularists, including secular Christians, who are unaware of biblical truth, may view those committed to biblical faith as irrational or Jesus freaks. They may think loyal followers of Jesus are foolish for trusting in the power of prayer and stupid to believe that Satan is alive and well. They unwittingly pressure us to avoid talking about painful truths, such as Satan, sin, Christ's shed blood on the cross, and what happens when we die. Furthermore, some in secular society impose an unspoken condition, that we not take our faith seriously, and if we do we are to keep it to ourselves. It takes courage for biblical Christians to live in secular society.

Secular Christianity Has Existed for a Long Time

Some in Secular Christianity (others may call it Cultural or Modern Christianity) think they are Christians, because they are Americans or because their parents were Christians. Still others reject biblical Christianity on philosophical differences, some of which seem valid to me.

Christianity's response to atrocities such as slavery in the United States or Hitler's ethnic cleansing give Secular society fuel for their inferno of philosophical differences.

Many in the Christian community agreed with, were involved in, or simply turned away from these tragic events. But Secularists aren't the only ones who abhor these examples of cultural calamities. I don't know of any biblical Christian whose head doesn't bow in embarrassment over such barbarity. They also ask questions such as, "How could our Christian forefathers let this happen?" or "Why didn't they stop it before it became a venomous lapse in moral decency?"

Power mongering and depraved thinking brought about by evil, hate, anger, and corruption are sins, and are the cause of such outrageous behavior. Usually, as in the case of Hitler, followers form a coalition of people who hold an idolatrous connection to the mastermind, a czar-like leader who has imagined a god that agrees with their arbitrary manifesto. As distorted and immoral as the leader's values are, they ring true for many supporters. Charismatic and brilliantly worded public speeches bring new people into the fold so they can learn about the "new" true church. We've all had experiences when we might have followed along just to hang out with the popular kids.

Dietrich Bonhoeffer (1906-1945), a German Lutheran pastor, theologian, and anti-Nazi dissident, was a key founding member of the Confessing Church, which opposed Hitler's agenda. As a pacifist, Bonhoeffer was involved in the underground movement against Hitler. After the Third Reich and the Vatican reached their concordant in 1933, and Hitler believed that he had won the church's approval, Bonhoeffer remained true to his Christian beliefs. Even after the Gestapo closed his seminary, Bonhoeffer continued to teach students and published his book *Life Together,* in which he shares his communal experience of living dangerously. Shortly thereafter, World War II started. As time passed, Bonhoeffer's Christian values led him to conspire with a Swedish friend to assassinate the Fuhrer. Arrested by the Gestapo and imprisoned in 1943, he later became the resident chaplain to his assigned concentration camp.

In his *Letters and Papers From Prison,* Bonhoeffer spoke about what he called "religion-less Christianity":

> *What keeps gnawing at me is the question, what is Christianity, or who is Christ actually for us today?*

The age when we could tell people that with words—whether with theological or with pious words—is past, as is the age of inwardness and of conscience, and that means the age of religion altogether. We are approaching a completely religion-less age; people as they are now simply cannot be religious anymore. Even those who honestly describe themselves as 'religious' aren't really practicing that at all; they presumably mean something quite different by 'religious.'

After spending two years in the concentration camp, the authorities hanged Dietrich Bonhoeffer—just days before the Allied troops liberated the prisoners. Telling Bonhoeffer's story is important to me for several reasons:

He lived his faith tenaciously and without compromise.

All people, including you and me, are susceptible to errant thinking when influenced by charismatic leaders and churches who try to lead us astray by reinventing God's purposes for humanity.

There are times, such as in World War II, that we must engage in a war.

Most importantly, Bonhoeffer's "religion-less Christianity" forms the background for the rest of this book.

The twenty-first century needs a non-religious response to the world, one in which we push empty, nonresponsive religion aside in favor of reasoned faith. The world needs to see more faith in action, where we become the hands and feet of Jesus and share his love.

Reflection Questions

1. Has someone in your family turned away from God? How did you feel about it, and what did you do?

2. Do you believe the rise in secularism is partly responsible for the decline in moral, spiritual, and political ethics in America? If so, why?

3. Or do you believe America is on the right path? If so, why?

4. How do you think your personal story fits into God's grand story of redeeming humanity?

5. What do you think about Sheila, who said her religion was an "–ism" of herself?

6. Explain what it means to be the hands and feet of Jesus in the world.

CHAPTER 2

Twenty-first Century Religion

I've been praying that we might have a spiritual awakening. But I think that becomes possible as individuals surrender their lives fresh and anew to Christ.

–Billy Graham

SIX VOLUNTEERS WERE planning a traditional Jewish Seder dinner for our congregation and invited guests. We wanted to replicate the traditional Passover celebration closely, and included the six Seder foods on each plate. Each food is symbolic of the 430 years in Egypt that the Israelites suffered in captivity before the exodus.

A lamb shank, the symbol of an unblemished lamb, represents the act of atonement for the Israelites' sin. The focus of our celebration was our own unblemished lamb, Jesus Christ, who atoned for our sins. One of the volunteers scoffed at our meticulous preparation as we searched for authenticity.

"Come on, do you really think they did all of that?" she asked.

"Of course they did," answered another volunteer. "It was the last Passover meal that initiated the Lord's Supper."

"Oh. I get it," she replied.

This is an example of how some Christians aren't aware of how the threads of the Old Testament weave themselves into the New Testament. In *Christianity is Jewish*, Edith Schaeffer wrote that the early Christians were all Jews, and some of them who read their Torah carefully, believed in and waited for the coming Messiah, Jesus Christ. They recognized and accepted him as the fulfillment of prophecy. Accordingly, in Hebrews we read about the connection between the blood of the Jewish Passover lamb and the blood of Christ.

But when Christ came as high priest of the good things that are now already here, he went through the greater and more perfect tabernacle that is not made with human hands, that is to say, is not a part of this creation. He did not enter by means of the blood of goats and calves; but he entered the Most Holy Place once for all by his own blood, thus obtaining eternal redemption. The blood of goats and bulls and the ashes of a heifer sprinkled on those who are ceremonially unclean sanctify them so that they are outwardly clean. How much more, then, will the blood of Christ, who through the eternal Spirit offered himself unblemished to God, cleanse our consciences from acts that lead to death, so that we may serve the living God (Heb. 9:11–14).

Christian churches don't pay the same attention to other Jewish celebrations because the Jewish Passover is the one significant event we replicate through communion in order to confess our sins. It reminds us of why Jesus spilled his blood to atone for our sins.

"Now I Know You're Religious"

In *Life's Too Short to Pretend You're Not Religious*, David Dark wonders if it's a compliment to call someone religious anymore, and feels sympathy for those who are characterized as "religious." We can be "religious" about anything: exercise, cooking, sports, money, social activities, reading, gambling, social networking, online games, television, and gardening. Accordingly, many biblical Christians feel offended when others refer to them as "religious."

My former next-door neighbor confronted me the first day I met her. "Now I know you're religious," she said. Leaving the statement to hang in the air, she just looked at me. Dumbfounded, I had no response. We exchanged pleasantries, and I retreated into my house thinking, "Why did she say that to me? I just met her." A couple days later, I realized what happened. Mutual friends thought it important to alert my next-door neighbor that I was "religious." That way, she could decide to stay away from me since many in society avoid religious people.

The persecution of Christians is rampant in many countries throughout the world, and many lose their lives for their faith. Persecution is subtler in America. We can encounter avoidance, ridicule, or sarcasm. When Christians feel snubbed or barely tolerated by their peer groups, they feel oppressed and rejected. Some may decide to avoid non-Christians in the future. That isn't what Jesus did, nor should we. As uncomfortable as these situations are, biblical Christians are comforted by Jesus' words, "If the world hates you, keep in mind that it hated me first" (John 15:18).

What We Believe About Ourselves Determines Who We Are

In a *Christianity Today* article, I read that some media pundits characterize evangelicals as white, suburban, American, southern, and Republican. Evangelicals in my church are also Hispanic, African American, Scandinavian, Asian, Indian, and Unaffiliated or Democratic voters. Instead of asking us what we believe, the media makes assumptions that aren't true. And although we need journalists to keep us informed, we shouldn't let them define us. Some believe we aren't influenced by the media, but we are.

Talk shows can become a hindrance to our identity when watched religiously, pun intended. I've heard Oprah Winfrey refer to her faith on her talk show often. Her quoted sayings from her show contradict each other. She says, "what God intended for you goes far beyond anything you can imagine," but then in another quote she says, "You alone are enough." Although the words, "you alone are enough," aren't necessarily about religion, they are antithetical to those of us whose faith relies solely on Jesus' death and resurrection and not their successes. Mixed messages such as these discourage total reliance on God, especially for women whose faith is faltering.

Although aligning ourselves with popular cultural trends is tempting, it ends in disappointment when the new trend fades away. Then we feel obliged to wait for the next one. To resist these appeals, we should find our identity in our belief system and self-awareness. What we believe about ourselves determines who we are, not what others think we should be.

There it is folks, evangelical or not, we must ask ourselves: what do we believe and who do we believe we are? The identities and labels we apply to people are usually assumptions. We presume to know what a person's Christian identity means, when in reality

Time Out

Is Islam the same as ISIS? The answer is no. Faiths are not violent; it's what people do in the name of their faith that creates violence.

we should ask them what they believe, and why they call themselves a Christian, a Jew, or a Muslim.

Some Human-Designed Religious Traditions Border on Superficiality

We Americans love our traditions, don't we? Throwing out the first pitch on baseball's opening day, football games on Thanksgiving, St. Patrick's Day parades. The greeting card industry looks forward to manufactured holidays such as Grandparents' Day, Graduation from Kindergarten Day, and Bosses Day. The same is true for certain religious traditions.

Many human-designed religious traditions backfire when built on superficiality, established church culture, and personal desires. For example, the annual Advent Dinner at my church was a treasured tradition. Volunteers hosted tables using their finest dishes and decorations. Invited guests included family and friends who shared a lovely meal, followed by a program featuring a speaker or music. We enjoyed fellowship over dinner, while ushering in the Christmas season with great joy and celebration.

However, over time the table decorations became a competition. Very few outsiders attended and it evolved into just another Christmas party in a church basement where alcoholic beverages weren't served. The Advent Dinner had become less about the birth of Christ, and more about the secular parts of the Christmas season.

Established church worship traditions may also lead us astray. We form attachments to things such as time of worship, type of music, and order of service. We say, "We've always done it this way." Without evaluating cultural changes, the church, focused on past successes, latches on to what it thinks is best, and stagnation occurs. We forget that God sends people to our church who are different from us, including Secular Christians. Regardless, our churches must preserve faith-established values and principles based on Scripture, without regard for cultural changes. Still, we sometimes embrace errant religious customs, such as annual holidays that represent Christianity.

For example, Easter has evolved from celebrating the risen Christ into a secular holiday. We attend church and afterwards, the children hunt Easter eggs filled with candy or money.

Christmas is another example. We live frenzied and full of angst from October through December, hoping to purchase the right gifts, while planning the perfect Christmas dinner. We literally spend over half a trillion dollars every year according to the National Retail Federation. And for what? We pay for the privilege of high stress, deep anxiety, and buyers' remorse when the bills come around in January.

Just think—what would half a trillion dollars do for children and families who live in poverty with no food or fresh water? What would happen if we instead relaxed and enjoyed the holiday, celebrating the birth of Christ? Jesus speaks emphatically about religious traditions in Matthew 15. The hypocritical Pharisees and state-appointed Scribes questioned Jesus:

> *"Why do your disciples break the tradition of the elders? They don't wash their hands before they eat!"*

> *Jesus replied, "And why do you break the command of God for the sake of your tradition?"* (Matt. 15:2–3).

Later, in Matthew 15, Jesus said, "'These people honor me with their lips, but their hearts are far from me. They worship me in vain; their teachings are *merely human rules'"* (Matt. 15:8–9, emphasis added). Blinded by our intelligence and prosperity, some of us see little need for changing our holiday traditions in order to help those who are different from us.

Time Out

How should we celebrate Christmas? It's easy to say relax and enjoy the holiday as a Christian tradition. The reality is, your holidays don't just include you. How do you help your loved ones see the beauty and comfort of focusing on Christ instead of presents? For example, is there another way you can celebrate the true meaning of Christmas through a shared experience, such as serving dinner at your local homeless shelter?

Jesus Loves the Sinner, but is Loathsome of Lukewarm Christians

In exile on Patmos Island, the apostle John wrote Revelation, the last book of the Bible. Written in apocalyptic style, John's visions in Revelation are perplexing. They seem wild, even grotesque at times. Nevertheless, the message of John's vision in Revelation 3:14–17 is clear:

> *"To the angel of the church in Laodicea write: These are the words of the Amen, the faithful and true witness, the ruler of God's creation. I know your deeds, that you are neither cold nor hot. I wish you were either one or the other! So, because you are lukewarm—neither hot nor cold—I am about to spit you out of my mouth. You say, 'I am rich; I have acquired wealth and do not need a thing.' But you do not realize that you are wretched, pitiful, poor, blind and naked"* (Rev. 3:14–17).

Note that Jesus is speaking to John through a vision that John is recording. Jesus is the Amen, the faithful and true witness, and ruler of God's creation. John's vision metaphorically describes Laodicea, and according to Robert H. Gundry the city was so wealthy that after the earthquake in 60 A.D., there was no need for financial aid. The Laodicean Christians were self-sufficient and lazy. They had become complacent about their faith.

Laodicea is an ancient example of the United States in the twenty-first century. Jesus' words, "So, because you are lukewarm—neither hot nor cold—I am about to spit you out of my mouth" (Rev. 3:16) are applicable to many calling themselves Christians today. Not merely a figure of speech, Jesus is saying that he is loathsome of lukewarm Christians—those who refuse to stand firm in their faith.

Standing firm in our faith may seem difficult. And sometimes we resist because it isn't in our comfort zone. We aren't ready to step out in faith when the world is reluctant to either believe in or accept our decision to follow Jesus. You've heard the sayings "the time is now" and "never put off for tomorrow what you can to do today." Speaking from experience, the longer we wait to make a stand for Jesus, the longer it takes to live beautifully in a broken world.

A Person Listens to the Gospel Message and Believes It

In the first five books of the New Testament, we see a bridge. On one side are the gospels, giving us detailed information about Jesus and his ministry while on earth. In the middle of the bridge, the apostles see Jesus lifted up into a cloud and ascending to heaven. On the far side, the Acts of the Apostles begin. The scene unfolds dramatically:

> *When the day of Pentecost came, they were all together in one place. Suddenly a sound like the blowing of a violent wind came from heaven and*

filled the whole house where they were sitting.
They saw what seemed to be tongues of fire that
separated and came to rest on each of them. All of
them were filled with the Holy Spirit and began to
speak in other tongues as the Spirit enabled them
(Acts 2:1–4).

Jesus promised the apostles they would receive power when the Holy Spirit filled them. Amazingly, when "all of them were filled with the Holy Spirit," (Acts 2:4) the Spirit not only filled the apostles, but all believers. Metaphorical details transport us to the ancient city of Jerusalem. The "blowing of a violent wind" symbolized the Holy Spirit while "tongues of fire," symbolized God's divine presence. An event of enormous magnitude had occurred. The Holy Spirit descended on all believers and filled them in one cosmic swoop of wind and fire. Astonished, some bystanders mocked the believers and accused them of drinking too much wine.

Applying this scene to the twenty-first century, try to imagine a group gathered to watch the movie, *The God Who Wasn't There*. Each person, refreshments in hand, settles in to see the movie.

As the movie begins, a violent rushing wind descends, and tongues of fire erupt.

"What's going on? the moviegoers cry out. As the wind subsides and the fire is but a match-sized flame, latecomers walk into the theater thinking, "What the heck is going on?" Some people flee the theater. Others leave their seats and walk to the stage. Forming a circle, they hold hands and pray. Those remaining in their seats look at the group on stage with suspicion, their eyes sharply narrowed. One giggles, then two or three more, a quiet laugh here and there, until shrieks of hysterical laughing drown out the worshipers. Chuckles accompany the words, "They must be drunk on wine." After the Holy Spirit descended in Jerusalem, Peter gave his first sermon. Unbelievers witnessing the event asked him what they should do.

> Peter replied, "Repent and be baptized, every one of you, in the name of Jesus Christ for the forgiveness of your sins. And you will receive the gift of the Holy Spirit. The promise is for you and your children and for all who are far off—for all whom the Lord our God will call."
>
> With many other words he warned them; and he pleaded with them, "Save yourselves from this corrupt generation." Those who accepted his message were baptized, and about three thousand were added to their number that day. (Acts 2:38–41).

Back to the present, the spokesperson, standing on the stage, communicates loudly and with authority, explaining that each one baptized in the name of Jesus

Christ would receive forgiveness of their sins and the gift of the Holy Spirit. Some in the theater listened, believed, and joined the group standing on the stage in the theater. That's how it works, a person listens to the gospel message and believes it. If we compare the church in Acts to the church in Laodicea we see a distinct difference: they are as apples to oranges, oil to water, black to white, religion to faith, living beautifully to living ugly. The people in the Acts Two church were living beautifully in a broken world.

Buying Food for the Soul and Not Eating It

Are we even aware when we assume a lukewarm stance to our faith? Possibly not. Still, it is a dangerous proposition for three reasons. First, we might treat our faith as a hobby, such as bowling. Or, sometimes we replace Sunday worship with a trip to the mountains and find ourselves worshiping God's creation, not God. The Bible is the best-selling book of all time with over six billion copies sold and distributed. Yet many of us don't read it. That's like buying food for the soul and not eating it.

Second, uninformed about what the whole Bible says, we may pick out parts of the Bible that we think are most appropriate for us, while ignoring the rest.

Time Out

Some may say, "But the Bible is so hard to read and understand!" That's understandable. However, there are translations and paraphrases such as *The Message* that are very easy to understand.

Spending adequate time in the Bible helps us mature in our faith. Still, we resist the idea of fitting ourselves into God's biblical framework. We don't want to change, even though transformation is what we need. This is just like dehydration, which, deprives our brain cells of oxygen, limiting our ability to think. We become dizzy, and think we might faint, when all we need is water. Yet we resist changing and retreat back to not drinking enough water. Third, sometimes we don't take the time to read our Bible. Our unfamiliarity with it can cause us to fall into that category of lukewarm Christian.

Last, with our faith falling toward the bottom of our priority list, the danger of falling away from God increases exponentially according to the degree of disregard we place on our faith.

A Relationship with God Doesn't Require Proof

Authentic faith requires activity. Thus, while the Holy Spirit feeds and nurtures our soul, we should respond by searching our soul so that the Spirit's guidance isn't wasted. Furthermore, by confirming our faith subjectively and objectively, we view the world and its changes intuitively, and equitably. In other words, we view the world through a faith that is spontaneous, yet impartial. Thus, our faith is confident, compelling, and trustworthy as we reach out to the world. People will trust us only when they believe our faith is authentic. It may seem that growing an authentic faith is too difficult, but learning to search our soul and listening to the Holy Spirit comes with time. We don't acquire authentic faith immediately after we submit ourselves to Jesus Christ.

Google gives two definitions of faith: "Complete trust or confidence in someone or something" and "strong belief in God or in the doctrines of a religion, based on spiritual apprehension rather than proof." The Bible defines faith as "Confidence in what we hope for and assurance about what we do not see" (Heb. 11:1).

Notice that the secular definition is broader, while the biblical definition focuses on faith in God. They both define faith from differing perspectives, and I am not suggesting that one is wrong, while the other is right. Still, a relationship with God doesn't require proof. It happens on its own as we respond to his love, mercy, and grace. On the other hand, we can have "complete trust or confidence in someone or something," such as friends and family members, co-workers, and teachers, even our pastors and religious institutions. Again, the more secular definition is a broader definition that tries to define faith in both the secular and spiritual realm.

Is God on Our Side, Or Are We on His?

In *The Culture of Disbelief*, Stephen L. Carter wrote that religion is a way of denying the authority of the rest of the world, while telling fellow human beings we won't consent to their will. Carter's words beg answers to these questions: Do we want the wills of others to determine what we believe? Is "political and social correctness" necessary for us to get along in the world?

Discussing politics in a book about faith might seem distasteful. However, discussions about faith and politics occur in the media, at political debates, and even at the dinner table. Further, it's important to observe how current political ideologies in the media and government affect our faith. Do they make us waver back and forth in our core beliefs? We must inform ourselves, not necessarily by the media, inflammatory debates, or politicians' rhetorical comments. Critical thinking, the process of gathering information from different sources, analyzing the data, and drawing our own conclusions, helps us weed out pseudo-religious words and phrases that aren't faith-based. Over time, we establish for ourselves how to apply our faith to politics, and often in unexpected ways. Never assume a conservative Christian will always vote Republican or a liberal Christian will always vote Democratic. It's a simplistic view of a very complex issue. Let's remember that political rhetoric concerning faith is just that, rhetoric. In addition, when we hear "God bless America" at the end of a political speech, let's not assume that the speaker has authentic faith, nor is faith the impetus for the sign-off.

In *God's Politics,* Jim Wallis brought up a good point about cultivating a solid foundation for applying politics in our public and private lives. Wallis wrote that Abraham Lincoln had it right—that we should not invoke religion and the name of God by claiming God's blessing and endorsement for national policies and practices, thereby implying God is on our side. Rather, we should worry whether we are on God's side. Wallis further points to the two ways religion entered public life in American history. The first way, claiming God is on our side, leads inevitably to triumphalism, self-righteousness, bad theology, and, often, dangerous foreign policy. The second way, asking if we are on God's side, leads to much healthier awareness such as penitence, humility, reflection, and accountability.

Nowadays, bringing religion into public life in a healthy way is unheard of. Do Abraham Lincoln's comments matter anymore? They should. But our current political pundits and media tell us what to believe and how to think, their way.

Furthermore, mixing faith with philosophies, political affiliations, and other peoples' mindsets is risky, because it diminishes our faith and makes us uncomfortable when others disagree. It's as if the maid of honor goes to the bridal shop with the future bride, her mother, and the other attendants. Everyone, including the bride, loves a certain gown, except for the maid of honor. Is she really going to disagree with them and ruin the day? With the ugliness of twenty-first century politics, why are we inclined to remain silent rather than voice a different opinion? Is it because we think we won't be heard? So be it. Let's remember the admonishments of the apostle Paul:

Do not conform to the pattern of this world, but be transformed by the renewing of your mind. Then you will be able to test and approve what God's will is—his good, pleasing and perfect will. For by the grace given me I say to every one of you: Do not think of yourself more highly than you ought, but rather think of yourself with sober judgment, in accordance with the faith God has distributed to each of you (Rom. 12:2–3).

Paul is telling us to think for ourselves, look at the verifiable facts, and refrain from listening to family, friends, and neighbors. It's also important to reaffirm our faith every day, and be humble.

Reflection Questions

1. Do we look at ourselves through the lens of our own sense of reality or reality itself? Please explain.

2. Why do we resist the idea of fitting ourselves into God's biblical framework?

3. Are we willing to look at ourselves with sound judgment? If so, how should we do it?

4. What do we think a healthy sense of self and wholeness means?

5. Is authentic faith only about ourselves? Please explain.

6. Does it seem worth the time and effort? If so, why? If not, why?

PART II

WHERE DO WE BEGIN?

There must be a beginning of any great matter,
but the continuing unto the end until it be
thoroughly finished yields the true glory.

– Francis Drake

CHAPTER THREE

Made in God's Image

You weren't an accident. You weren't mass produced. You aren't an assembly-line product. You were deliberately planned, specifically gifted, and lovingly positioned on the Earth by the Master Craftsman.

— **Max Lucado**

"HOW COULD YOU even touch that man?"

"Oh, I probably know him," Nancy laughed. "Maybe I've seen him at the Samaritan House."

Leaving the Cathedral Basilica of the Immaculate Conception after a wedding, my friends and I were walking to our cars when a man approached us. Toothless and unkempt, reeking of body odor, his face caked with dirt, his clothes grimy and torn, the old homeless man smiled. Then he reached his hand out, not for money, but to shake someone's hand and feel the warmth of another person. My friend Nancy grabbed his hand, shook it compassionately, and gave him a wad of bills.

Next, he came to me. As his hand reached out to me, I turned the other way. How could I have done that? How could I?

The destitute man and I, both molded and patterned by God are equals in God's eyes. Yet, the man's cordiality and my cruelty showed two different hearts: one filled with love, the other with contempt. Nancy, a friend whom I believed had never gone to church, showed God's love, mercy, and grace to the derelict, while I pulled my hand away. She knew more about loving a distasteful person than me. No wonder some people want nothing to do with Christians and think they are hypocritical. Looking back on this incident, I cringe. In the meantime, I've learned to be grateful for the details of creation because they give me hope. Knowing that God created me in his image, motivates me to show friendliness and respect to people like the homeless man, because of what I learned when I first read Genesis 1:26–27:

> *Then God said, "Let us make mankind in our image, in our likeness, so that they may rule over the fish in the sea and the birds in the sky, over the livestock and all the wild animals, and over all the creatures that move along the ground." So God created mankind in his own image, in the image of God he created them; male and female he created them.* (Gen.1:26–27).

Notice the pronouns "us" and "our." I read the passage several times, and a thought occurred to me, "They were all there—the process was more complicated than I originally thought. Did the Son and Spirit give the Father advice? Or did they all agree since they are so intimately held together as one being?" Astonished, it occurred to me that all three watched me rebel those many years ago, and their collaborative work had challenged and changed me to be different. Now I try to look at all people as God's created beings who've simply lost their way, just like me. Choosing empathy and love over apathy and hate gives us the ability to view others as beautiful despite the brokenness of the world.

Time Out

How do we show God's love, mercy, and grace? Think about how you treat people every day. Not just the important ones like family and friends, but those you likely won't ever see again: the bagger at the grocery store, the receptionist at the doctor's office, the cable guy who shows up two hours late, the person who zoomed into your parking space. It's not just treating others the way you'd like to be treated; it's treating everyone you meet like they are special.

God Has Commissioned Us to Present His Image to the World

The fact that God created us in his image means that we resemble and represent him. This enormous and humbling responsibility requires that we show the world God's love, mercy, and grace. And although we feel inadequate, our faith is emboldened to learn and grow.

In his letter to all people of faith, Peter inspires and encourages us:

> *His divine power has given us everything we need for a godly life through our knowledge of him who called us by his own glory and goodness. Through these he has given us his very great and precious promises, so that through them you may participate in the divine nature, having escaped the corruption in the world caused by evil desires* (2 Pet. 1:3–4).

In addition, Jesus instructed the disciples to:

> *"Therefore go and make disciples of all nations, baptizing them in the name of the Father and of the Son and of the Holy Spirit, and teaching them to obey everything I have commanded you. And surely I am with you always, to the very end of the age."* (Matt. 28:19–20).

Known as the Great Commission, Jesus' instructions apply to you and me. That's not to say that we are all baptizers or teachers, but we are called to view the world as God's mission field, whether the field is next door or in another country. By accepting God's invitation to participate in his divine nature, we can respond beautifully to the brokenness in the world. We would do well to remember that just because we participate in God's divine nature doesn't mean that we are exactly like him. We are still sinners. Nevertheless, as we grow in intimacy with God, we find ourselves responding to all that he is.

God Doesn't Force Us to Grow

We are the pinnacle of God's creation. He gave himself to us and we are his dearly beloved. Still, to claim we are worthy of such a relationship is a bit reckless. Instead, let's respond to God by loving him as our dearly beloved. God has provided limitless resources that teach us how to show his imprint on the world; these resources are referenced in the list below.

Wisdom

Considered in Scripture to be the wisest man in the world, Solomon's writings found in Proverbs, teach us to apply divine wisdom to daily life and provide moral instruction. Solomon refers figuratively to Wisdom as a woman who guides us and helps us succeed.

Original Righteousness

In Ecclesiastes 7:29, Solomon says, "This only have I found: *God created mankind upright*, but they have gone in search of many schemes" (emphasis added). That God created man upright, points to a moral disposition of original righteousness. Notice that Solomon also acknowledges we've gone astray. We need to tap into the power of the Holy Spirit within us and receive God's righteousness.

God's Character

The "image" or "likeness" of God includes some of his attributes, such as love, grace, and mercy. These are seeds of himself instilled in us as human beings at creation. As noted above, we must use those traits in how we respond to others.

Instead of forcing us to grow, God expects us to use these resources by responding to him as his dearly beloved children. Apart from the above intrinsic resources are spiritual disciplines, such as meditation and solitude. In Chapter 8, we will explore how they deepen our faith and intensify our love relationship with God.

In *Opening up Genesis*, Kurt Strassner reveals the four D's that tell us what it means to be a human being created by God:

Dignity

Because God creates everyone in his image, no one should suffer from degradation, nor should the destruction of humanity come about through social injustice, prejudice, sexual abuse, abortion, or euthanasia.

Dominion

God gave us a mandate to rule over the earth and other creatures in a responsible way.

Distinction

God created males and females equally in the image of God, but their roles are distinctly different.

Duty

Our relationship with God is not between equals nor is it autonomous. We are dependent on God and accountable to God in our service and obedience.

In addition to the four D's, God placed within us a "God-shaped vacuum" and an inherent desire to fill it, a need so severe, that we search incessantly and sometimes fill it with things like sex, alcohol, drugs, or unhealthy food, only to realize that God alone can fulfill the void.

A Perfect Relationship Does Not Exist in This Life

The Father worked with the other members of the Trinity at creation. Yet, the idea that each person in the Trinity is fully God seems unfathomable. The more we try to understand it, the less we know. Thinking about them as the "triple crown" of the Christian faith might help us remember their mutual indwelling. I don't intend to be flippant when I use triple crown, and there is no biblical reference. But sometimes it helps us to make a mental picture of something to remember it, especially something as complex as the Trinity. For me, the triple crown metaphorically represents a solid band of gold with three points, representing all three Persons at work in unison with one another, committed to their communal relationship and us. There is symbolism behind my mental picture of the crown that represents life; eternal life!

In James 1:12 we read, "Blessed is the one who perseveres under trial because, having stood the test, that person will receive the crown of life that the Lord has promised to those who love him." The Trinity created us and will be with us for eternity in some form or another. Thus, we should avoid the inclination to think of only God the Father as being all knowing, all-powerful, and eternal.

While God the Father spoke the words of creation, the Son came to earth in human flesh, taught us how to live, and restored fellowship between God and humanity. The Holy Spirit enabled the prophets to foresee the future, taught our ancestors, and led our spiritual leaders; he now lives in us, shaping us into God's image. In Matthew 3:16–17, we see a good example of how the Trinity works individually and together.

As soon as Jesus was baptized, he went up out of the water. At that moment heaven was opened, and he saw the Spirit of God descending like a dove and alighting on him. And a voice from heaven said, "This is my Son, whom I love; with him I am well pleased" (Matt. 3:16–17).

At Jesus' baptism, the Father spoke, and the Spirit descended, clearly demonstrating the unity and diversity of God. As the Trinity lives unified as one God in a perfect relationship, we might ask, then why can't we?

A perfect relationship on earth doesn't exist, because of our inherited sin. Yet memorable moments spent with family around the dinner table or rich conversations shared with others in our faith might give us a tiny glimpse of a perfect relationship. Perhaps the best example is the intimacy shared between husband and wife. Still, even in that earthly relationship, the perfect love that flows within the Trinity is unparalleled, because we don't place God as the head. Think of it this way: a marriage triangle in which God is at the top point. When both the husband and wife look to God and draw closer to him, they draw close to each other.

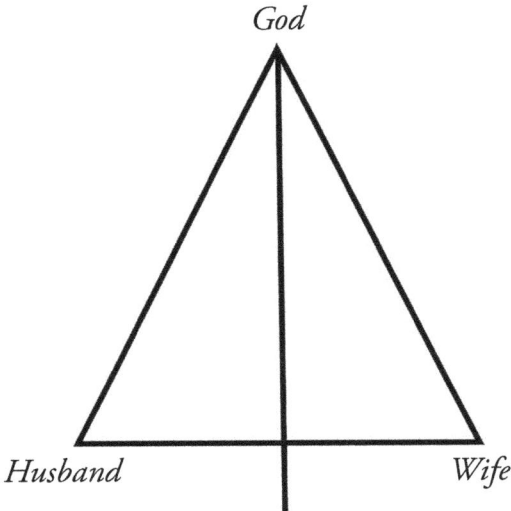

God

Husband   *Wife*

God's Image Involves Man's Essence and Not His Function

At fourteen, bored, and home alone, I decided to drive my mother's car. It was a 1956 Chevy hardtop, bronze, and cream in color, with a leather interior and white walled tires. It looked like it would be fun to drive. Justifying this crazy and dangerous scheme was easy; I thought, "Well if she can drive it, then I can drive it . . . besides, they left me at home alone again, so I can do whatever I want, right?"

I called some friends that were a bit timid, but after some finagling, I finally convinced them to come along. Excited and slightly fearful, I believed I was living the dream. We drove to a drive-in movie and concluded our escapade with a trip to Berry's, a drive-in restaurant. As I mentioned earlier, I always wondered if I would ever please God enough for him to make plans for me. This flawed thinking made me believe that God would make plans for me, when I cleaned up my act. As a curious, rebellious, know-it-all, I failed to discover that God had already made plans for me. I figured there was no hope for me, so I tried to balance myself on a fine line between walking the straight and narrow and nearly jumping off a cliff.

In *Mansions of the Heart*, Thomas Ashbrook explains that spiritual formation begins, for better or worse, even before a person becomes a Christian. Further, while the influences of sin, death, and Satan attempt to warp the soul, the Holy Spirit calls out to us, using whatever means are available. This means that from the day we are born the Holy Spirit works as an agent of change in us, while God watches over us, and protects us from ourselves. Thankfully, God's compassion prevails when we make harmful, life-altering decisions. Still, there are consequences—and many times, we suffer from shame and embarrassment.

But Phillips, Brown, and Stonestreet's book *Making Sense of Your World: A Biblical Worldview* gives us hope. The authors explain that God's image involves man's essence and not his function, which means that His image is associated with who we are, not what we do.

God's Divine Image is in Man and God's Divine Relationship is with Man

It's important to remember that God's image never leaves us. Hence, just as he pursued Adam and Eve after they sinned, God wants to commune with us, even when we make mistakes. Nurturing our relationship with God is more important than any other relationship, even marriage. Caring for our relationship with God makes all other relationships healthier in a holistic way.

We are the final stroke on God's creation canvas. Therefore, we should affirm that humankind is distinct from the rest of creation. Remember that God commissioned us to "Rule over the fish in the sea and the birds in the sky and over every living creature that moves on the ground" (Gen. 1:28). God's instructions about our role in caring for his creation are "to rule," so it isn't surprising that we sometimes fail.

Therefore, when we compare God's intentions for his created beings to the secularist view, that man's experience has nothing to do with the supernatural, we see very quickly how humanity has lost its way. If God's purposes for humanity don't mean anything, then how can we expect the world to be any different from what it is? God created us to be different, to be ministers of reconciliation in the universe. As Adam and Eve brought sin into the world, God's plan is to use Christians to make the way of redemption known to the world. God initiated his plan and when we focus on his plan, we recognize our own need for redemption and we see the brokenness of the world differently.

We don't need to raise our hand, hoping God will grasp it. He reaches down and brings us to him, restoring us through his grace. It's as simple and perplexing as that. Paul, a former persecutor of Christians, tells us how God's redemption worked for him:

> *But by the grace of God I am what I am, and his grace to me was not without effect. No, I worked harder than all of them—yet not I, but the grace of God that was with me* (1 Cor. 15:10).

Paul is talking about salvation, given through God's grace. The idea that we don't earn our salvation is alien to us. We think we are productive, prosperous, and self-sufficient. Admitting that we can't restore our relationship with God requires humility. More importantly, salvation *rebuilds* the fullness of God's divine image *in* man and God's divine relationship *with* man.

Some may ask, "So what's the use? If we can't fix ourselves, why bother?" The point is that God "fixes us" and makes us new by conforming us to his image twenty-four hours a day, and acknowledging this, brings us peace, relief, and renewal.

Vaclav Havel (1936-2011), the first president of the Czech Republic wrote, "The tragedy of modern man is not that he knows less and less about the meaning of his own life, but that it bothers him less and less." Havel's tragedy of modern man isn't about what we know, it's about what we should want to know. It begs us to answer basic questions. What is the meaning of my life? Why am I here? Do I have any value? More importantly, reading between the lines of Havel's observation, three other questions might stand out:

Do we ever ask ourselves complex questions about our being?

If we do, how do we respond?

Do we even care what the answers are?

In other words, if we don't know from one day to the next what we should identify ourselves with, how can we begin to raise questions about why we are here or why we exist? The lack of existential substance in our culture is the result of turning away from God's plans and purposes for his creation. Furthermore, we are all responsible. We brought ourselves to this point of discontent and frustration by rejecting God. So, what can we do? Is there a way to turn back the clock? Where do we go from here?

Trying to solve the puzzle of what our lives mean should cause us to question our value and purpose. No one figures this out for us. It takes courage to identify the specifics of how our lack of direction guides us. A variety of characteristics may lead us astray: a secretive personality, the lack of a moral upbringing, a rebellious temperament. Regardless, when channeled with godly motivation, they help us fulfill God's purpose for our lives.

For example, God created me fearless. Ready to try anything at a moment's notice, I don't mind being in the spotlight. Hesitant to acknowledge these somewhat brash characteristics about myself, I know they exist. My point is that once I began walking with Jesus earnestly, these personality traits emboldened me. They helped me plunge into the Bible, to study, and do the work necessary for facilitating or teaching Bible studies, to go on mission trips in Eastern Europe, and to start college for the first time at age sixty-seven and graduate with honors. In writing this book, God is using me for his purposes and he will do the same for you. All of this isn't because of me. It's God and his ability to make me into a new person solely through faith in him.

Once we embrace our essential kinship with God, our specific character traits lead us to purposeful living, our life's tapestry. And the richness of our tapestry evolves from our raw materials. In *Mere Christianity*, C. S. Lewis wrote, "God does not judge a man or a woman on the raw materials at all, but on what he or she has done with them."

Some people grow up in an unstable environment, some feel like losers because of the way their parents talked to them, or maybe a person has suffered from abuse. These are the raw materials, and God is less interested in how these raw materials have worked against us, and more interested in how we take them and use them for good. For example, many women who have suffered from domestic abuse, leave the relationship and become well known speakers at conferences and schools to educate those women who still struggle and haven't had the courage to leave the relationship.

Twelve Billion Neurons Are Poised for Action at Birth

"Oh, you can look later. They'll still be there. Right now you should rest," Dad said to Mom after my birth. Mom wanted to count my fingers and toes. Dad didn't want her to see my club foot. Resting on mom's pelvic bone in the womb throughout the pregnancy, after my

birth my right foot settled at a sharp angle to the left side
of my ankle, much like a golf club. Was my birth defect
God's mistake? Of course not. Recall Ps. 139:13–16:

> *For you created my inmost being; you knit me
> together in my mother's womb. I praise you because
> I am fearfully and wonderfully made; your works
> are wonderful, I know that full well. My frame
> was not hidden from you when I was made in
> the secret place, when I was woven together in the
> depths of the earth. Your eyes saw my unformed
> body; all the days ordained for me were written
> in your book before one of them came to be*
> (Ps.139:13–16).

Written by King David, the language in this passage
describes God's limitless power over the creation of
humanity. Awestruck, David's fundamental knowledge of
the human body caused him to praise God for supervising
our psychological, inward parts (mind and emotions),
and physical structure (our frame) during our creation.
Doubters exist.

The original Hebrew word for "inmost being" refers
to the kidney, what the Jewish people understood at that
time as our temperament, heart, mind, spirit, and seat of
thoughts and emotion. Similarly, "knit" refers to God's
direct activity in the growth of the fetus. The phrase, "you
created my inmost being and you knit me together in my

mother's womb" clearly demonstrates God's concern for our psychological and physiological health.

In *Fearfully and Wonderfully Made*, Philip Yancey and Dr. Paul Brand point out significant aspects of how God created our bodies. The pelvis of a man is quite different from the oval shaped opening in a woman's pelvis. And while childbirth explains that anomaly, there are other ingenious details in regard to our muscular structure and its activity. Created with robust strength and masterful control, afferent neuron cells carry messages to our brain, while efferent neuron cells control our muscles. Amazingly, twelve billion neurons are poised for action at birth. Our minds cannot imagine how God strategically placed all of these elements to work so perfectly in our bodies. Concepts such as these and the mysteries surrounding God's creative processes are eternal truths that we view through the eyes of our faith. No other explanations are found or needed, for that matter.

In closing this chapter, I am reminded of King David's words, "Your eyes saw my unformed body; all the days ordained for me were written in your book before one of them came to be" (Ps. 139:16). Then later, in the New Testament, the author of Hebrews wrote:

> *God also bound himself with an oath, so that those he promised to help would be perfectly sure and never need to wonder whether he might change his plans.*

He has given us both his promise and his oath, two things we can completely count on, for it is impossible for God to tell a lie. Now all those who flee to him to save them can take new courage when they hear such assurances from God; now they can know without doubt that he will give them the salvation he has promised them. This certain hope of being saved is a strong and trustworthy anchor for our souls, connecting us with God himself behind the sacred curtains of heaven, where Christ has gone ahead to plead for us from his position as our High Priest, with the honor and rank of Melchizedek (Heb. 6:17–20, TLB).

Our connection to God remains a mystery to the human mind. However, our faith guides us to the truth. God not only created us, but also promised to never leave us, and has given us an anchor for our soul.

Reflection Questions

1. What were the circumstances behind a time when you felt God was reaching out to you?

2. To what extent do you ask yourself complex questions about your being? What are they and how much time do you think about the answers? Explain how your answers fit your life.

3. What does it mean to you when C. S. Lewis wrote, "God does not judge a man or a woman on the raw materials at all, but on what they have done with them"?

4. What are your thoughts about the mechanics of how God created us, such as the difference between a man and woman's pelvis?

5. If you had to describe one aspect about yourself that you absolutely love, what would it be?

CHAPTER FOUR

Self-Awareness

Your vision will become clear only when you can look into your own heart. Who looks outside, dreams; who looks inside, awakes.

– Carl Jung

PRETENDING TO BE someone we aren't shows a lack of self-awareness. It also causes embarrassment. On one such occasion, my husband and I were unloading our bikes at the base of a mountain. Single-track trails circled the mountain edges, which we were going to ride for the first time. As novice riders, we didn't want to spend a lot of money on heavy-duty bicycle helmets. Instead, we purchased Styrofoam helmets along with the heavy netting that stretches over them to keep the Styrofoam intact in case of a fall. The helmet-shaped nets had animal heads painted on them; my husband's had a dinosaur and mine had a dragon (I know how funny this sounds). To make sure our helmets faced the correct direction for safety, we always put the netting with the animal's head to the front. Ready to push my bike up to the trailhead, I noticed an obviously experienced rider, quite attractive in his spandex, coming down the mountain. As he approached us, I put my dragon helmet on.

"How was the ride?" I asked.

"Great," he answered.

"We can't wait to get up there," I said as I smiled.

"Uh . . . your helmet's on backwards," he said with a grin as we pushed our bikes passed him.

I laugh hysterically now—but at the time, I felt like crawling under a bush. I wanted the other rider to think I was an experienced off-road cyclist.

Self-awareness is Three Dimensional

The story about riding our bikes was funny, but Peter calls us to a much deeper level of self-awareness:

> The end of all things is near. Therefore be alert and of sober mind so that you may pray (1 Pet. 4:7).

Peter's advice applies to how we view ourselves, relate to others, and prepare for Christ's return. He encourages us to take prayer seriously and to reflect on the changes we need to make, knowing that Christ's return is imminent. Essentially, he has instructed us to be spiritually self-aware. Self-awareness is three-dimensional in how we view and recognize our authentic selves.

Self-awareness requires:

An objective evaluation of our life story: our experiences, what we hold dear, those events in our lives that grab our attention, our actions, and reactions to the world around us

An understanding of how our life story influences our behavior and how others respond to and view us

Consideration of these two dimensions through God's perspective and what changes we need to make as a result

Researching ourselves involves the above exercises, even though circumstances and major life changes, such as death or divorce affect how we feel. We are not static creatures. Our hearts and souls constantly evolve as we navigate through life. Therefore, the questions we ask ourselves change during the research phase of becoming spiritually self-aware. The essence of who we are, how we relate to the world, the way we think, live, and respond to society, comes from knowing ourselves through God's eyes, even when it's painful.

We Can Look at Ourselves in One of Two Ways
The first dimension (authentic evaluation) is sometimes difficult, because we might view ourselves with contempt over our past. After I became a Christian, I lied.

I was ashamed of my past, so when sitting alongside other Christians, guilt prevented me from telling the truth. For example, I couldn't imagine myself meeting someone for the first time, shaking their hand, and saying, "Hi, I'm Carol. I've been married three times, and have three children from my first husband, one from my second, and my third husband took pity on me and adopted my children as his own." And yet, that's my story. The courage to stop lying came from the fact that I only needed to please God, not other people. Furthermore, he already knew my story and still loved me.

Lying about our past can cause our relationship with God to collapse under the burden of guilt as we subconsciously distance ourselves from him. Fortunately, we can deal with our past. Journaling helps us look at and verbalize heartaches, failures, and past mistakes. We learn to know ourselves better, and change our perspective about who we were, who we are, and who we want to be. Interestingly, we can look at ourselves in one of two ways. We can look at ourselves from below (horizontally), through man's perspective or from above (vertically), through God's perspective.

In the horizontal view, we may see ourselves as just another blip on the radar screen of life, or as someone with inflated importance; it depends on the person. Regardless, egoless and egotistical people are usually self-involved. Dissatisfied, the egoless person concentrates too much on their image, while the egotistical person is distracted through self-absorption. Either way, a view of self from man's perspective isn't sufficient, because we don't have answers to our questions or the answers we hear are wrong.

In the Bible, the story of Job illustrates how we can agonize over ourselves while searching horizontally for meaning in our lives. Looking at himself in despair, Job didn't understand God's dealings with him. Miserable and in pain, he wanted answers from God about his predicament.

> *"I loathe my very life; therefore I will give free rein to my complaint and speak out in the bitterness of my soul. I say to God: Do not declare me guilty, but tell me what charges you have against me. Does it please you to oppress me, to spurn the work of your hands, while you smile on the plans of the wicked? Do you have eyes of flesh? Do you see as a mortal sees? Are your days like those of a mortal or your years like those of a strong man, that you must search out my faults and probe after my sin— though you know that I am not guilty and that no one can rescue me from your hand?"* (Job 10:1–7).

Immersed in himself, Job wallowed in self-pity and blamed God. He temporarily endangered his faith by questioning God and forgetting about God's essential faithfulness. He wrongly assumed that his innocent suffering meant that God had abandoned him. In the end, however, Job was restored, once he re-evaluated his position before the Lord.

Viewing ourselves vertically takes us back to creation. God created each of us as unique individuals, while making all of us the highest point of creation, and uncommon from the rest of creation in a collective way. Unalike physically and mentally, God gave us certain personality traits, different viewpoints, interests, and ideas. And although we sometimes neglect or misuse our one-of-a-kind qualities, he doesn't tally our sins and hold them against us. Instead, he changes us, not just once, but throughout our lifetime.

Knowing that God endowed us with unique qualities and wants to transform us, helps us understand why turning to our earthly friends for answers isn't always effective. And although we need friends, they don't know us as God does, nor are they capable of knowing our thoughts. Which is why looking at ourselves vertically is best.

We Can't Escape the Frayed Fabric of Our Inherited History

To understand our personal history, we must review our inherited history. Although we are essentially singular and special, distinct from one another in every way, we must deal with the sobering situation from which we all came. Original or ancestral sin is part of who we are, whether we like it or not.

In his book, *The Pursuit of God*, A. W. Tozer wrote an accurate analysis of our "real spiritual trouble":

> *There is within the human heart a tough, fibrous root of fallen life whose nature is to possess, always to possess. It covets things with a deep and fierce passion. The pronouns my and mine look innocent enough in print, but their constant and universal use is significant. They express the real nature of the old Adamic man better than a thousand volumes of theology could do. They are verbal symptoms of our deep disease. The roots of our hearts have grown down into things, and we dare not pull up one rootlet lest we die. Things have become necessary to us, a development never originally intended. God's gifts now take the place of God, and the whole course of nature is upset by the monstrous substitution.*

Tozer's "real spiritual trouble" relates to and demonstrates how sin manipulates us. Just observe Eve in the Garden of Eden:

> *When the woman saw that the fruit of the tree was good for food and pleasing to the eye, and also desirable for gaining wisdom, she took some and ate it. She also gave some to her husband, who was with*

her, and he ate it (Gen. 3:6).

Tempted, Eve desired what she saw and ate it, despite God's command not to eat it. There you have it, pure and simple, temptation and desire, the precursors to sin. Like Eve, we are tempted, desirous, and we take. Consequently, God's gifts replace God.

We can't escape the frayed fabric of our inherited history. Nevertheless, as mentioned earlier, God doesn't focus on our raw materials, but what we do with them. Therefore, our hope for a godly life comes from his desire to transform us and bring glory to himself. When we are mindful of our inherited history while observing our personal history, a wonderful change in our perspective occurs. Our melancholy feelings shrink while joyfulness expands, and our embarrassment fades while self-confidence shines. In other words, once we own our human nature (the inborn tendency to sin), we can scold ourselves moderately over our past misdeeds, while learning about who we really are, wholly loved children of God.

Once we decide to view ourselves vertically (from God's perspective), we begin to explore our spiritual "birth knowledge," which means that we have reconciled ourselves to our inherent sinfulness at our birth, by immersing ourselves in our beginnings as unique children of God and then look back to our personal history. In *Courage and Calling: Embracing Your God-Given Potential*, Gordon Smith advises us to look at our personal history if we want to know ourselves. "But, how does my personal history explain me?" we ask.

As a young adult, I never understood why I felt inferior, always trying to impress other people, combative, needy, and negative. Through journaling and reflection, I concluded that low self-esteem had fostered unhealthy feelings within me. Growing up, I struggled with wetting my bed. Whenever I had an accident, my dad called me "stinky" for the day. Mom called me "sweetie," but for some reason, that didn't remove the stench of Dad's nickname. Later in junior high school, when my grade point average slid from straight A's, down to two A's, two B's, and one D, my dad, a successful businessman said, "Well you're just a dumbbell like me."

Unraveling these incidents helped me see myself through God's eyes as his wonderfully created daughter. It also softened my attitude toward my earthly father, because I knew my heavenly Father loved both my earthly father and me unconditionally. During childhood, we normally encounter different types of unintended hurts from our parents and others. Indifference, bravery, and ignorance toward painful childhood experiences are damaging in adulthood, because they may result in unresolved anger. However, confronting our feelings about them brings closure and courage.

We might also need to separate ourselves from learned sin and behavioral patterns, but that doesn't mean turning away from our earthly family. Jesus said, "If anyone comes to me and does not hate father and mother, wife and children, brothers and sisters—yes, even their own life—such a person cannot be my disciple" (Luke 14:26). Jesus isn't telling us to hate our family members. He is instructing us to love him more. Loving Christ above all earthly people humbles us and makes us aware of the magnitude of our relationship with him and all of humanity.

The creation story paradox reveals itself as we see ourselves in the bigger picture. Try to think of yourself as one star, in one galaxy, in the observable universe, in which more than two trillion galaxies exist. Although each of us is unique, significant, and wholly loved by God, we are but a minuscule part of God's brilliant and divine story. We must be willing to pursue our own history as a microscopic dot in the most important story of all. When we do this, we will find ourselves morphing into genuine people who live and breathe in true harmony with ourselves and others. When we live in alignment with our beliefs, we are unafraid to tell the truth about ourselves, and we express our true feelings about our beliefs, even those that are unpopular with family, friends, and

Time Out

How do I express my true feelings about my belief system? As simple as it may sound, expressing the truth about our belief system becomes natural, because God has given us permission to do so. Next time you find your inner voice telling you to say something or defend someone, go for it! That's called freedom!

society.

We Need to Separate Who We Think We Are, From the Truth of Who We Really Are

By resuscitating myself many times over I was reluctant to know myself. I didn't know where to start. Encouraged by a sermon, *God Doesn't Make Junk*, I began sorting myself out, and although I didn't know it at the time, my lengthy evaluation of myself became a form of spiritual self-awareness. From reading the Bible, I understood my value, purpose, and that God had plans for me.

> *"For I know the plans I have for you," declares the Lord, "plans to prosper you and not to harm you, plans to give you hope and a future. Then you will call on me and come and pray to me, and I will listen to you. You will seek me and find me when you seek me with all your heart"* (Jer. 29:11–13).

In this passage, God spoke through Jeremiah to the captives in Babylon. Hananiah, a false prophet, disputed Jeremiah's prophecy that Israel would spend seventy years in captivity by saying it would last only two years. Naturally, the people wanted to believe Hananiah. The sixty-eight-year discrepancy compelled Jeremiah to send a message of truth to the captives. An unpopular message, it required Jeremiah's raw courage, conviction, and grit to tell the exiles the truth, that they would be in exile for seventy years.

Imagine that you are addicted to alcohol. Your friend Susan writes to you saying that God has plans for you, plans that will not harm you. Then Susan tells you to seek God and stand against Mary, another alcoholic who encourages you to stay on the path of bondage and betrayal.

Susan values you and sees you destroying your life. Out on a limb, Susan fears you will abandon the friendship, but she still tells you the truth, knowing that you will suffer before you get better. At that turning point in your life, you must separate who you think you are (a social drinker), from the truth of who you really are (an alcoholic), who is nevertheless a child of God. By understanding what being a child of God can mean to your life, hope for overcoming your alcoholism springs anew.

Our Attention Collection is Serious Business

Looking back at my "before Jesus" life, I'm aware that whimsical dreams, lackadaisical ideas, and undefined thoughts filled my mind. The events, memories, and grandiose ideas I'd given my attention to during my lifetime had accumulated into what David Dark calls an "attention collection." Dark explains in *Life's Too Short to Pretend You're Not Religious*, that an "attention collection" is a "book of common things, [a] working palette of lifelong recognitions." Our own lifelong recognitions involve life experiences that teach us something about ourselves. They can be positive or negative. In either case, a review of our attention collection can help us acknowledge the truth of who we were and who we are today.

And while everything in our lives up to this point makes our attention collection what it is, questions remain. How will it inform us in the future? What memories or events should we obliterate? Can we expunge those recognitions that harmed us and replace them with something good? These informational pieces are elusive, because they change and grow over time. Recent cultural shifts, such as lack of time and civility, create havoc in our attention collection. Much of what we see, hear, and read floats in and out of our consciousness.

Newspapers, encyclopedias, and network news have morphed into convoluted news apps on cell phones, E! News, and Wikipedia. Well thought-out letter writing has evolved into quick, sometimes-inflammatory emails, texts, and tweets. And although I enjoy the convenience of online research, email, and writing this book on my computer, I refuse to investigate many media outlets. My filters are set against topics like the Kardashians, how to make bombs, and sexually charged reality shows. But what about young adults and teens, whose brains aren't fully mature? Filling their minds with one obscenity after another, some have become immune to decency and the sanctity of life. They may have an alibi for filling their attention collection haphazardly. But what about those of us over the age of twenty-five? We have no excuse.

Our attention collection is the unspoken repertoire from which we build our moral, social, and faith worldviews.

Our attention collection is not something we share casually, if at all. It begins with a personal inventory of what we paid attention to in the past, what we pay attention to now, and what we want to pay attention to in the future. And although we don't always discuss our thoughts with others, our actions reflect how we see ourselves. Most important, however, is that God knows our every thought.

Recall again, God walking in the garden and looking for Adam and Eve: "But the Lord God called to the man, and said to him, 'Where are you?'" (Gen. 3:9). Ancient history shows that although God is privy to our every thought and action, he still wants to be in relationship with us. Our response to this cosmic phenomenon is to toss out the negatives and fetch the positives in our attention collection often and in whatever way works for us. This activity will enhance our relationship with God.

We can be True to God's Purpose for Us and Remain True to Ourselves

Since we are what we think, and our actions reflect our thoughts, journaling is a good way to begin cultivating our attention collection. Daily devotionals pave the way for journaling. We study a Scripture reference or subject, we reflect on it, and write down our thoughts. It takes just a few minutes, and we often surprise ourselves at what we learn.

Many times, while journaling in Oswald Chambers' *My Utmost for His Highest* daily devotional, I learned something new about myself. For example, in a reading about being "Placed in the Light" (December 26), Oswald wrote, "The evidence that I am delivered from sin is that I know the real nature of sin in me." Part of my response was this, "When I look back on my life before Jesus, I am truly embarrassed by my darkness in behavior. That's because I'm walking in the light! Praise God!"

Eventually, we realize that at one time or another our filters eroded, they were never consciously activated or re-booted, and we subconsciously allowed unhealthy ideologies to invade our thought life. Then we begin the real work. We must ask ourselves, how did I get here from there? What was I thinking? Is this

Time Out

How do I purge the negative? Purging isn't automatic. It takes a conscious act to get back on track, much like someone trying to quit smoking may snap a rubber band against their wrist every time they realize they're craving a cigarette. When I get something in my mind that's unhealthy, I put my hands together in front of me, as if I'm holding the unhealthy thing in my hands, and I lift it up, as if to say, "Please take it, God." And he does. Now that may sound silly, but the physical act is what makes the difference. In this case, where the body leads, the mind can go.

what I really want in my attention collection? Fleshing out these details takes time and effort. But, if we seriously want to know ourselves, a review of our attention collection can be very informative. It sounds like a lot of work. Our days are stressful, rushed, and long. We don't want to think, we want entertainment. However, when we identify problematic areas that aren't in our best interest, and purge them, we free ourselves from cultural coaxing, unhealthy notions, and habits. Purging the negatives involves recognition of the problems in our lives followed by giving the problems up to God through prayer and confession.

When we keep God's purpose for our lives in mind, we learn to make reasoned, independent choices using our intellect, which is often sizzling on the back burner. We can be true to God's purpose for us and

Time Out

How do I de-compartmentalize my life? Compartmentalization makes the complexities of our life worse. De-compartmentalization provides not only a holistic view of our life, but a consistent compass that provides direction. A good example of applying the Bible to the whole of our lives is constantly asking ourselves the question (though it may seem trite), "What would Jesus do?" in whatever situation we find ourselves. For example, if a cashier gives you too much change, by silently asking yourself what would Jesus do, you know you need to give it back.

remain   true   to   ourselves.

We admit our failings and flaws, we leave our "before Jesus life" behind, and put our trust in God's purpose for our "after Jesus life."

However, some people compartmentalize their minds. It supposedly helps us cope with the demands of work amid family needs. This modern phenomenon looks great at first glance, but it threatens our mental and emotional health. By dividing certain issues in our minds, such as politics from

Further, applying the Bible to the whole of our lives helps us cultivate and nourish our attention collection. Once it's refined and reviewed, we recognize it for what it is: an armory filled with memories, thoughts, observations, and knowledge of who we are at our core. Then we are standing on higher ground.

religion, it seems easier to keep track of them. Partitioning our mind into neat little boxes causes us to lose our sense of self and wholeness. Since we are complex people with complicated problems, an undivided life helps us cope in all circumstances and makes us holistically healthier.

Reflection Questions

1. If you were to interview yourself, what would your first question be?

2. When has embarrassment and shame plagued you? What did you do about it?

3. What is your view on how we might punish ourselves too harshly as we apply original sin to our lives?

4. Tell about a time when you looked back on life and said, "If only." What were the circumstances? Explain how you might begin creating an attention collection.

5. If you compartmentalize your life, what are your compartments? What, if any, undeveloped compartments exist? What will you do to find out? And to what extent will you continue with the habit after reading about it?

PART III

NOMINAL RELIGION OR AUTHENTIC FAITH?

*If you don't feel strong desires for the
manifestation of the glory of God,*

*it is not because you have drunk deeply
and are satisfied.*

*It is because you have nibbled
so long at the table of the world.*

*Your soul is stuffed with small things,
and there is no room for the great.*

— John Piper

CHAPTER FIVE

Nominal Religion

There is within every soul a thirst for happiness and meaning.

– Thomas Aquinas

THE VIOLINIST ISAAC STERN once spoke on *The Today Show* about his good friend, Irving Berlin, shortly after Berlin passed away. Stern described the songwriter's philosophy of life as simplistic, comprised of three existential phrases, "life and death, love and loneliness, hope and defeat."

At first glance, we might see two opposing lives: life, love, and hope — or death, loneliness, and defeat. One may be described as pleasant, the other as bitter. Did Stern's assessment of Berlin's philosophy of life mean that our lives must be one or the other? Of course not. Our lives are complex and filled with conflicting experiences, emotions, and uncertainty. Furthermore, perceptions about life, our own or another's, depend greatly on our view of ourselves, culture and its changes, the world, and subsequent consequences.

From the moment we are born, we snuggle into our mother's breast and want the warmth and comfort of that human connection to last forever. However, as we grow up, our lives, satisfying or mundane, leave us longing for more. Our everyday existence has periods of loneliness and defeat, no matter who we are. Illness, divorce, loss of a loved one, financial stress, and distrust of the government take their toll. Despite what we may think, these hardships are nothing new.

Time Out

How do I have faith that God has a plan for my life when something awful happens? We seek solace through a Christian friend; we pray and we cry; we recall the stories about Noah, David, and Paul, and how God brought them through trials. We look back at our history with God and the times he watched out for us, even when we were unaware.

In some ways, the violence, tyranny, and ignorance to the teachings of Christ thousands of years ago are similar to today's woes, because differing opinions about interpretations of the Bible brought chaos into a graceless society. Furthermore, Christian scholars and leaders suffered ridicule, and in some cases, lost their lives. So, as we look at the disconnect between nominal religion and authentic faith, let's not forget what we've learned about Christian history, ourselves, human nature, and the world around us.

We Don't Just Become Christians, We Become Children of God

"Religiosity" is another word for religious excess. We see it in the behavior of hypocrites and pious, judgmental people. Pointing their fingers, or turning away from a derelict like I did, they criticize anyone whose values don't fit theirs. A hypocrite preaches one thing and does another. Self-righteous and obsessed with looking virtuous; pious and judgmental people don't usually sit at the table of reason and reality. And yet, we all carry the religiosity banner at one time or another. Jesus addressed the Pharisees in the same manner that he addresses us.

> "You're hopeless, you religion scholars and Pharisees! Frauds! You're like manicured grave plots, grass clipped and the flowers bright, but six feet down it's all rotting bones and worm-eaten flesh. People look at you and think you're saints, but beneath the skin you're total frauds" (Matt. 23:27–28, MSG).

The term "religiosity" applies to people whose faith has shifted away from God in favor of religion. Driven by individualistic beliefs, many focus on acting religious, while allowing their relationship with God to take a subordinate role, the opposite of God's desire. He wants us to follow him, not promote religion, to engage in a new life, not a new religion.

In *Letters and Papers from Prison*, Dietrich Bonhoeffer disagreed with human religiosity as the focal point of sharing the gospel message. In other words, people who share their faith should set religiosity aside and focus on Jesus as the way to salvation. Our focus should be about how a personal relationship with God changes us, not how religious we are.

Do we want our faith to shine a spotlight on religious rules and rituals, human ideology, and self-appointed beliefs? Or do we prefer to immerse ourselves in a life-giving relationship with our Creator who changes us and makes us new? Baptism, being a good person and citizen, obeying the law, and sharing our resources with the poor could be strong indicators that a person has a relationship with Jesus. On the other hand, those particularly Christian endeavors do not constitute a relationship with the living God when they aren't motivated by true faith. Hence, when we submit to Christ, we don't become religious Christians, we become children of God.

Trying to be in Control Only Hurts Us

When I first became a Christian, my life didn't change as I had hoped. Not long after my conversion, it seemed as if our business was falling apart. "Why is this happening to me?" I sobbed as I laid my head down on the kitchen counter. "Why is God allowing this to happen?" I wondered. "What have I done to deserve this?"

The computer programmer promised it would take three days to get our business system up and running after an upgrade, but it took three weeks, which dramatically changed my workload. The first week, I was irritated, ready to blow my stack. The second week, frustration bordering on hysteria set in. By the third week, I wavered between screaming at the top of my lungs and sobbing uncontrollably off and on for hours at a time. I tried to do all the work manually, but there was no way to keep track of inventory, which adversely affected daily operations. I couldn't control the situation. I exploded several times a day, often without warning.

Throughout this traumatic and unproductive three-week period, I felt like my faith was sinking in the quicksand of self-pity. I believed God was punishing me so I brought him into the equation of my predicament for the first time in my life. In a convoluted way, I tried to blame God, because I thought I needed punishment for my prior misdeeds and sins. I doubted his forgiveness, love, mercy, and grace. "Haven't you punished me enough?" I asked.

Running a small business with a malfunctioning computer system in a big world is but one example of how I lost control while trying to gain it. It didn't work then and it doesn't work now. Trying to control everything in life is futile and only hurts us. We don't understand, we question God, we wring our hands in frustration, but nothing works to relieve our angst. These negative emotions hurt us by lowering our energy, becoming stressful, grumpy, not interested in family life, and most important causes our faith to falter.

I believed that working hard and keeping my nose to the grindstone would bring fewer tribulations and more triumphs in my life. That didn't work in my business, and it didn't work in my faith journey either. The world order and our faith collide when we compare working for a paycheck to accepting the free gift of salvation.

Only after I surrendered my life to God, did I begin to understand that my work, sweat, and tears weren't what he wanted from me. And although I had accepted the gift of salvation, I believed I must toil for God to keep it. That wrong notion nearly destroyed my love for him. When I attended a Bible Study called *Breaking Free: Making Liberty in Christ a Reality in Life* by Beth Moore, it helped me "break free" of the work ethic I had grown up with, and God "bound up my broken heart, brought me to freedom, and released me from the darkness" (Isaiah 61:1, my paraphrase).

Misguided clichés and pet doctrines tend to trivialize authentic faith and are good examples of how nominal religion can slither in and destroy authentic faith. For example, have you ever heard

Time Out

Breaking Free: Making Liberty in Christ a Reality in Life is still available, which I recommend to anyone who is suffering from emotional turmoil brought about by low self-esteem, unresolved anger, and shame from their past.

anyone declare, "God helps those who help themselves" or "Everything happens for a reason"? Sometimes, even when God is involved, we don't know his reasoning, but usually, idiomatic phrases like these are not biblical. Still, when we hear false but cleverly worded phrases, we easily believe them as truth. These phrases can make us mad, are divisive, and can easily lead us astray, causing disunity in the church. Those promoting pet doctrines might say they are gospel-driven, but often, they are interested in creating a gaggle of cohorts who will support them.

Assuming Our Sins Don't Matter Because We're Saved is Superficial Faith

Our brief understanding of hypocrisy, religiosity, the need for discernment, and surrendering our lives to Jesus is only the beginning. The Bible provides simple and straightforward guidance on how to live. For example, the book of Proverbs provides what we call "life skills." King Solomon, known for his wisdom, tells us:

> A troublemaker and a villain, who goes about with a corrupt mouth, who winks maliciously with his eye, signals with his feet and motions with his fingers, who plots evil with deceit in his heart—he always stirs up conflict. Therefore disaster will overtake him in an instant; he will suddenly be destroyed—without remedy (Prov. 6:12–15).

In this passage, it appears Solomon is describing a naughty boy. On the other hand, he could be metaphorically depicting an adult who is insincere and loves conflict.

The story of Job is distinct from Proverbs, because we are privy to a conversation between God and Satan as the drama unfolds:

Then the Lord said to Satan, "Have you considered my servant Job? There is no one on earth like him; he is blameless and upright, a man who fears God and shuns evil. And he still maintains his integrity, though you incited me against him to ruin him without any reason."

"Skin for skin!" Satan replied. "A man will give all he has for his own life. But now stretch out your hand and strike his flesh and bones, and he will surely curse you to your face."

The Lord said to Satan, "Very well, then, he is in your hands; but you must spare his life" (Job 2:3–6).

In other words, the Lord held Job in his highest esteem. But Satan challenged God, saying the only reason Job was "blameless and upright" was because of his wealth. Confident of Job's faith, God gave Satan permission to test him, but not kill him.

Satan inflicted painful sores on Job's body, a rival tribe stole his livestock, and another tribe killed his children. Yet he refused to curse God. Three of Job's friends mourned his losses with him and sat in silence for seven days and nights. Job's pain was so unimaginably horrible, that he cursed the day he was born. Then after the week of silence, his friends chastised him without mercy, saying these things wouldn't have happened had he not sinned in some way. But Job knew he was innocent. Job told his accusers, "Your memorable sayings are proverbs of ashes [. . .]" (Job 13:12, NASB).

Job could see the errors in his three friends' statements as they tried to put the hood of "superficial religion" over his eyes and called them out. Those who try to twist God's will and spread false doctrine are hypocrites. Their concern is not about true and deep faith, but about money, popularity, and a way of boosting their self-esteem. Sometimes the media covers "doomsday believers" who say they know exactly when the world will end. What better way to get free publicity than to promote oneself by distorting God's Word, which clearly states no one will ever know the time.

When we rebel against God, we try to guide ourselves. Many times, that seems to work perfectly. However, in God's eyes, our rebellion, no matter how small, is incorrigible. Our sin separates us from God, because he cannot tolerate sin. Nevertheless, we have an abiding hope found in John 3:16, "For God so loved the world that he gave his one and only Son, that whoever believes in him shall not perish but have eternal life."

Still, we rebel. Some immature Christians and unbelievers take a "ho hum" approach toward their rebellion and sin. To assume that rebellion doesn't matter, because we're saved or know that salvation is available is superficial faith.

We Are Not the Judge

Many supposed religious rituals, rules, and traditions created by Christian men and women border on legalism. In Colossians 2:20–23, Paul taught about the danger of strict adherence to the law, rather than the spirit of the law.

> *Since you died with Christ to the elemental spiritual forces of this world, why, as though you still belonged to the world, do you submit to its rules: "Do not handle! Do not taste! Do not touch!"? These rules, which have to do with things that are all destined to perish with use, are based on merely human commands and teachings. Such regulations indeed have an appearance of wisdom, with their self-imposed worship, their false humility and their harsh treatment of the body, but they lack any value in restraining sensual indulgence* (Col. 2:20–23).

In this context, Paul is teaching those who were authentically converted to Christ.

In today's culture, Paul might have said, "I know it's a hard thing to do, but you shouldn't live 'socially and politically correct,' because you are now living a new life in Christ Jesus." When we keep "correctness" at the forefront of our minds, we walk the beaten path of doing life as others see fit and expect others to do the same.

By pushing our own version of God's perfect law, we assume we are above the law, as if *we are* the judges. Typical of C. S. Lewis, he injects a bit of humor in the section about the Christian rule of chastity in *Mere Christianity*. Lewis wrote, "That is why a cold, self- righteous prig who goes regularly to church may be far nearer to hell than a prostitute. But, of course, it is better to be neither." Yes, it is better to be neither.

Time Out

How do I avoid political correctness but still live in grace and truth? We decide for ourselves what our core beliefs are, and in discussion with those who oppose our beliefs, we remain committed, but kind. We also become familiar enough with the Bible that we can point to certain biblical facts that support our view. Just remember, the world hated Jesus first (John 15:18).

Distractions Disappear When We Keep our Eyes on Jesus

Sometimes, we only remember Paul as the apostle God chose to bring the gospel to the Gentiles. Interestingly, when he persecuted Christians, his given name was Saul.

> *As he neared Damascus on his journey, suddenly a light from heaven flashed around him. He fell to the ground and heard a voice say to him, "Saul, Saul, why do you persecute me?"*
>
> *"Who are you, Lord?" Saul asked.*
>
> *"I am Jesus, whom you are persecuting," he replied.*
>
> *"Now get up and go into the city, and you will be told what you must do."*
>
> *The men traveling with Saul stood there speechless; they heard the sound but did not see anyone. Saul got up from the ground, but when he opened his eyes he could see nothing. So they led him by the hand into Damascus. For three days he was blind, and did not eat or drink anything* (Acts 9:3–9).

Such a commanding and cosmic event is puzzling. Why did God allow Saul to endure blindness for three days? Was it because he persecuted the Christians? Of course not. God's purposes are far more powerful and intentional than senseless retaliation. God used Saul's blindness to remove all visual distractions. Hence, Saul spent three days seeing himself persecuting the Christians. He responded by looking to Jesus only. And after a few days, he began preaching that Jesus Christ was the One and Only Son of God.

Of course, most don't have such a momentous experience when they convert, but the fact remains that once we look only at Jesus to govern our lives, we can't help but respond in a similar way. Try to picture yourself at the starting line of an Olympic race. With the stadium filled, you look up and see hundreds of family and friends watching you. Suddenly, in the collage of faces, you see Jesus. At that moment, wouldn't you spontaneously look only at him? If we keep our eyes on Christ, we'll follow him humbly and obediently, trying to adopt his attitude. In Philippians 2:5–8, Paul describes how this should work for us.

In your relationships with one another, have the same mindset as Christ Jesus: Who, being in very nature God, did not consider equality with God something to be used to his own advantage; rather, he made himself nothing by taking the very nature of a servant, being made in human likeness. And being found in appearance as a man, he humbled

*himself by becoming obedient to death— even death
on a cross!* (Phil. 2:5–8).

Did you notice the words, "in your relationships with
one another?" God's desire for relationship, his with us
and ours with others, is reiterated throughout the Bible.
When we commune with the living God, we respond
organically. Without even thinking about it, we receive his
humility and love, and share it with all other people as
best we can.

Time Out

How can we respond
organically when we
commune with God? We
rely on the Holy Spirit
as our conscience. You
would be amazed at how
much we underutilize
this one dimension of
ourselves (our conscience)
in a life of chaos. It's
because we've lost that
child-like innocence that
guided us before we
could see the brokenness
in the world.

Authentic Faith Requires More Than Feelings

As our cultural contexts
on relationships have changed,
some of us have changed our
views about a relationship
with God. Unfortunately,
faithfulness and commitment
aren't held in as high regard
anymore. Some people can fall
in and out of a "committed
relationship" every other
month or so. Hence, a
human love relationship
pales in comparison to a love
relationship with God. So, for
this cosmic "love relationship,"
it's important to understand

love in the context of faith.

The essence of our love for God and his love for us is hard to unfurl. Infinite and inspiring, it takes our breath away once we commit ourselves. Called "agape" in the Greek New Testament, it is the highest form of love, and brings delight to our souls. Sensual and stimulating, our "sacred romance," based on love for God, flourishes when we draw near to him.

Loving God isn't like loving a human. When we frustrate him, God doesn't pout. He doesn't have an automated voice system. God is always listening. He hears us when we are melancholy, angry, or frightened; he hears us when we are ecstatic, cheerful, or courageous. And even though we aren't always honest and steadfast, God's truthfulness and faithfulness remain. In Genesis 9, we read:

> *And God said, "This is the sign of the covenant I am making between me and you and every living creature with you, a covenant for all generations to come: I have set my rainbow in the clouds, and it will be the sign of the covenant between me and the earth. Whenever I bring clouds over the earth and the rainbow appears in the clouds, I will remember my covenant between me and you and all living creatures of every kind. Never again will the waters become a flood to destroy all life* (Gen. 9:12–15).

Rainbows appear naturally in the midst of rain clouds. But when we see one and think about God's faithfulness to his vow, an ordinary rainbow takes on new meaning, because God told Noah it is the sign of his promise for all generations to come. Looking at a rainbow, I can't help but "feel" my faith.

Nevertheless, listening to inspiring music, like the "Hallelujah Chorus" from Handel's Messiah or the late Leonard Cohen's "Hallelujah" may elicit an emotional response, but our passion for the music doesn't sustain our relationship with God. If that were the case, when the music stops, our passion would go with it. That's not to say we should stifle our feelings. If we don't allow ourselves to experience our faith emotionally, we lose the richness of our relationship with God and we're less effective in sharing our faith with a broken world.

It's difficult not to apply faith to human situations. When I have struggled with serious health concerns, such as a recent brain aneurysm, my first response was that God had providentially watched over me, by keeping the aneurysm from rupturing. How could I not have felt my faith in that situation? Nevertheless, authentic faith requires more than feelings. Channeling those feelings into action will support the biblical reasoning behind our faith, even when it's a ministry of inconvenience.

Does Christianity Have to Change with the Times?

We often hear that Christianity needs to "attract new believers and accommodate progress in scientific thinking." Although we want to affirm our faith intelligently, we run the risk of allowing modern cultural trends to obscure the timelessness of the gospel's core message. Not just a passing fancy in today's world of religion, most theological liberals claim that a reconstruction of belief is essential for Christianity to remain a serious intellectual option for knowledgeable people. In essence, they argue that Christianity needs to change with the times. The tendency of the modern world is to reconstruct religion anew with wide-ranging diversity instead of submitting itself to the unique authority of Christ.

Furthermore, reconstructionism is engaged in religious ambition rather than spiritual worship, and refuses to take on the burden of talking about sin. They'd rather take their cue from today's talking heads and pundits who need to continually come up with a "new" message to stay relevant. Accordingly, some Liberal Protestant churches

Time Out

How do I apply the Word of God without reconstructing my beliefs? The short answer is, you can't. Your reconstruction of belief is the opposite of the reconstructionist, who is ready to change God's word. You are making an inward change that informs your beliefs as you apply God's word to your life.

readily surrender distinctive Christian doctrines to become acceptable to contemporary culture.

In my opinion, reconstruction of belief is unacceptable to our faith, because as noted above, the emphasis on self unseats Christ as Lord of our lives. That said, applying the Word of God to certain aspects of culture are necessary, because not doing so goes against the ministry of Jesus. Remember that Christ placed himself in the cultural settings of his day to teach and minister to all peoples. Jesus touched the untouchable (Luke 5:13), he talked to the Samaritan woman at the well who had been married five times (John 4:7–17), he ate with sinners (Matthew 9:10–12), he never looked down on others (Matthew 18:10–14), and he let a sinful woman pour perfume on his feet (Luke 7:36–38). In each of these

Time Out

Is the "All Lives Matter" movement diametrically opposed to "Black Lives Matter"? No, it isn't. Black, Asian, Native American, Hispanic, all lives, fall under the phrase "All Lives Matter." An unarmed black man's death by a police officer could indicate racism (sin) and presupposed fear (sin, due to racism and unreliable historical contexts). The Christian response to this type of incident is sorrow for both the victim and the officer. Also, we respond by not judging, unless that's the way we make our living. The value of putting Christ into the culture, as the culture exists, cannot be overstated.

cultural settings, Jesus adapted to the situation to create an opportunity to teach spiritual truth.

People of faith should respond in a like manner. We must bring the message to the culture. We must not change the message to fit the culture. Above all, we must accept the culture as it is. Our commitment to reach out to all communities is not negotiable. All lives matter and it is our responsibility to engage with people individually or in their community.

Reflection Questions

1. What does it mean to suffer from the loss of warmth and comfort in our lives?

2. How does our self-awareness help us see the depravity in the world around us and ourselves?

3. Have you ever felt frustration that bordered on hysteria? Tell us about it.

4. Tell about a time when you rebelled and tried to take your life into your own hands.

5. Did you grow up in "correctness," letting your parents tell you how to do life? If so, how did it affect you as an adult?

6. How do you apply your faith to human situations? Does it come from emotions or reason?

CHAPTER SIX

Authentic Faith

When we come to the end of ourselves, we come to the beginning of God.

–Billy Graham

OUR EXCURSION THROUGH secular society, twenty-first century religion, creation, self-awareness, and nominal religion has transported us to a life bridge. In the deep ravine below, men and women stagger through life, never grasping the realities of why the world is morally, spiritually, and politically bankrupt. Perhaps they once stood on the human side of the bridge. Not understanding themselves and the world, these men and women might have been reluctant to cross over into the cosmic relationship that comes from drawing near to the living God.

Authentic Faith Strives to Live What it Believes and Stands the Test of Time

Society's view of Christianity has changed drastically. It's perceived negatively by many and rejected by some.

However, since our authentic faith experience is unique and personal, it's best to ignore the media and other people's opinions. We should not try to compare or criticize another person's faith journey. Hence, when we claim to know God, our lives prove or disprove what we believe. Jesus explains this in the following ways:

> "[. . .] *by their fruit you will recognize them"* (Matt. 7:20).

> *"Make a tree good and its fruit will be good, or make a tree bad and its fruit will be bad, for a tree is recognized by its fruit"* (Matt. 12:33).

> *"No good tree bears bad fruit, nor does a bad tree bear good fruit. Each tree is recognized by its own fruit. People do not pick figs from thornbushes, or grapes from briers"* (Luke 6:43–44).

Jesus' metaphorical language may confuse us, but the substance of what he means is unparalleled. He is contrasting two types of people. Do we want to obey or reject the One who died for us? The tree illustrates us and our faith determines the fruit. Therefore, if the nature of the tree is good, plenty of good fruit grows. However, if we are spiritually barren, there will be only bad fruit. Those people who give the appearance of piety but remain far from God will bear bad fruit or no fruit at all. Their trees (chopped down) become kindling for the fire. Only those whose hearts grow into godliness, obedience, honesty in words and actions, and live by the Holy Spirit remain close to God and bear good fruit. We must remember, "[. . .] the fruit of the Spirit is love, joy, peace, patience, kindness, goodness, faithfulness, gentleness, self-control; against such things there is no law" (Gal. 5:22–23, NASB).

Our faith is authentic when we grasp the reality of the Bible and live accordingly. By viewing everything we experience through our faith, we recognize our sinfulness, repent, value humility, and know who we are in Jesus. We live in this broken world, but we resist the temptation to become a part of the depraved culture it offers. Nevertheless, we love the world as God does and we try to live beautifully today, in anticipation of eternity where no brokenness dwells.

In addition, authentic faith stands the test of time. A person with authentic faith doesn't put their tail between their legs and run away when life takes a bad turn. They stick with it. Paul, who encountered many

Time Out

What does it mean to bear bad fruit or no fruit at all? Bearing bad fruit, or adding to the chaos and brokenness of the world, is the person who shoplifts or (at the other extreme) murders a child. In God's eyes, each of these behaviors are evil because they represent a person who has rejected him. A person who bears no fruit is uncaring and disinterested in the brokenness of the world.

trials, spoke from experience, "And not only this, but we also exult in our tribulations, knowing that tribulation brings about perseverance; and perseverance, proven character; and proven character, hope [. . .]" (Rom. 5:3–4, NASB). In Hebrews 12:1, we read about the "great cloud of witnesses" who've gone before us, and the writer of Hebrews inspires us by telling us that we are not the first to struggle and that others have run the race and won.

Authentic faith makes us strong. Our hope for the future never fails, because we are confident, unafraid, and believe in God's promises. True faith is an eternal love relationship with God that makes us whole in mind, body, and spirit. And because we love God above all others, our life is full of him. Our response to this mystical, life-altering adventure builds over time until it becomes natural, like breathing.

However, for many of us who attend church regularly but are still searching for answers, God may not be our primary focus. When we are involved in Bible study and see the ways God has revealed himself, it's like a courtship. As we get to know the Lover of our souls, we love him back. The more time spent on our relationship with him, the more committed we are to loving God above all others.

Still, some of us trivialize the heart adjustments the Holy Spirit makes in us. Perhaps we've developed a sense of spirituality within ourselves. We may perceive that spirituality is the same as authentic faith or listening to celebrities, new-age church pastors, and well-known authors who expound on how we should be searching for the sacred within ourselves. We supposedly encounter our own "inner self," achieve personal growth, and enjoy euphoric significance in our lives.

My husband and I witnessed this type of spirituality at a fundraiser to aid research for an incurable illness our friend suffered from. We sat at a round table with six other people and listened to a message given by a new-age church pastor. Near the end, he asked all of us to "reach out for your inner self" by thrusting our arms upward, forefingers pointing to the ceiling. The other people thrust their arms upward, but we kept our hands folded on our laps beneath the table. We did not mean to disrespect our friend and his religious preferences, but we were uncomfortable participating in such a self-propelling spiritual affectation.

Spirituality is an ambiguous word. However, its synonyms, "immateriality," "otherworldliness", and "unearthliness" point to God, not people. In *Systematic Theology*, Wayne Grudem wrote, "God exists as a being not made of any matter, with no parts or dimensions that we cannot perceive through our bodily senses, and is the most excellent kind of existence." Even though we want to talk about and recognize our spirituality, our existence isn't the same as God's. We're not on the same spiritual, intellectual, or comprehensive level as him.

When we engage in a loving relationship with God, we turn from superficial spirituality and self-love to reverence and reality. We see the unbelieving world as God does, corrupt, evil, and sinful, yet love it. We focus on relating to the world as it is. We choose to engage in the possibilities that come from a smile, handshake, hug, or kind word.

We admit that changing ourselves may help to transform the world, but we also recognize it is worrisome. For example, how often do we want to change something about ourselves, but not too soon? An authentic faith life is not easy. A constant battle in our soul rages. The apostle Paul explains:

I don't understand myself at all, for I really want to do what is right, but I can't. I do what I don't want to—what I hate. I know perfectly well that what I am doing is wrong, and my bad conscience proves that I agree with these laws I am breaking. But I can't help myself because I'm no longer doing it. It is sin inside me that is stronger than I

Time Out

How do I love a world that is corrupt, sinful, and evil? It comes down to realizing that any one of us is capable of corruption, evil, and sin to a degree. Nevertheless, God loves us.

We can follow God's example by getting up each morning and asking, "Do I want to love others today, or do I want to sit back, complain, and judge them?" You make the choice. Although gruesome stories surround us every day, our choices can change how we respond to them.

*am that makes me do these evil things. I know I am
rotten through and through so far as my old sinful
nature is concerned. No matter which way I turn
I can't make myself do right. I want to but I can't*
(Rom. 7:15–18, TLB).

Still, God accepts us as we are, and waits patiently
for us to surrender to him. He gives us the benefit of
doubt, by acknowledging we don't always know better.
Peter wrote, "As obedient children, do not conform to the
evil desires you had when you lived in *ignorance*" (1 Peter
1:14, emphasis added). God dwells in us on both sides of
our struggle and he is with us always.

Our Father's House Has Many Rooms

Looking historically at God's preparations for the
coming of Jesus Christ provides ample assurance that
he is preparing the way for us. Isaiah tells us that a voice
calls us to clear the way for the Lord and smooth out the
desert highway for our God (Isaiah 40:3). Three hundred
years later, Malachi reiterated Isaiah's message when he
wrote:

*"I will send my messenger, who will prepare the
way before me. Then suddenly the Lord you are
seeking will come to his temple; the messenger of
the covenant, whom you desire, will come," says the
LORD Almighty* (Mal. 3:1).

Finally, John the Baptist cleared the way, baptized many, and preached that baptism would only come after repentance. In addition, the prophecy and events leading up to the birth of Jesus compel us to trust that God prepares the way for us, helps us become more like Christ (the process Christians refer to as "sanctification"), and prepares us to enter into his presence.

The disciples spent approximately three years following Jesus. They were comfortable in his presence, but when he predicted his betrayal, they couldn't understand why Jesus had to leave them.

Simon Peter asked him, "Lord, where are you going?"

Jesus replied, "Where I am going, you cannot follow now, but you will follow later."

Peter asked, "Lord, why can't I follow you now? I will lay down my life for you" (John 13:36–37).

The disciple's despondency over losing Jesus came from the fact they had been with him physically, day and night, for over three years. Paradoxically, our doubts and fears come about because we don't have him with us physically. Still, our feelings are just as extreme. "If only I could touch Jesus," we say. We can't touch him, but we can count on him. Jesus assured us of this:

"There are many homes up there where my Father lives, and I am going to prepare them for your coming. When everything is ready, then I will come and get you, so that you can always be with me where I am. If this weren't so, I would tell you plainly" (John 14:2–3, TLB).

Yes, we wish we could touch Jesus and talk to him, but that isn't God's way. God wants to see our faith in action as we walk a different path from the world. As aliens and sojourners, we will never feel at home on earth. Nevertheless, we abide in Christ, and as the writer of Hebrews explains, we long for a better country, a heavenly one. "And God is not ashamed of us, he has prepared for us a city" (Hebrews 11:16, my paraphrase). Paul gives additional assurance about God's wisdom concerning his preparations for us:

No, we declare God's wisdom, a mystery that has been hidden and that God destined for our glory before time began.
None of the rulers of this age understood it, for if they had, they would not have crucified the Lord of glory. However, as it is written:
"What no eye has seen, what no ear has heard, and what no human mind has conceived"— the things God has prepared for those who love him— these are the things God has revealed to us by his Spirit.

The Spirit searches all things, even the deep things of God (1 Cor. 2:7–10).

God is preparing a place for those who love him.

Our Heart is the Seat of Emotions, Affections, Intellect, and Will

Just as God prepares a place for us, we must respond by preparing a place for him in our hearts. God created a thirst for him in us, and that craving depletes us, because we search endlessly for love, acceptance, and contentment in all the wrong places, but never find what we are looking for. But God satisfies in phenomenal and unexpected ways.

How Does Your Garden Grow?

We each have a garden
That God has designed to grow
It's in our heart... deep within
It's the pulse of life as it flows

When the Father knits us in the womb
He makes our garden lush and fertile
But as we grow up surrounded by the world
It becomes parched, barren, and brittle

God gives us desire to bring it back
We long for a watered soul

But Satan sows pain and sorrow
He dares us not to be whole

His plan is for wasteland
To wither and wilt away
Can our garden in love exist?
When Satan plants every day

Living Water is what we need
It will nourish and sustain our days
Our garden's earth will start to soften
Refreshed and redeemed, we explore new ways

As the Water begins to give new life
Within the center of our soul
A pool of clarity and purpose gathers
An oasis that will forever flow

This Living Water comes only from Christ
When we seek Him for all of our needs
It never stops flowing in our heart
As we prepare to accept perfect seeds

Some of the seeds are of righteousness from truth
They must be planted throughout our garden
The Holy Spirit will sow the first seed
That because of Christ we are pardoned

Other seeds become plants of discipline
The Holy Spirit prunes and shapes them
The flowers give sweet, sweet smells of joy
Petals once faded are now precious gems

All other seeds will find a place
With Living Water to nourish and sustain
The seeds in our garden grow into Him
A garden of purity will be our gain!

Our garden becomes a sacred harvest
As others reap from the precious seeds
God is the only One who knows
To what destiny each harvest will lead

As you can see in the poem I wrote, tending our garden nourishes it and affects our behavior. And our authentic response to Jesus' promised eternal life creates a sense of urgency to tend our garden now. By observing the unbelieving world as God does (corrupt, evil, and sinful, yet loving it), we find the strength and empowerment to live expectantly, as though Christ's return is just moments away.

Authentic Faith Requires that we Make a Choice to Follow Jesus

With our will governing our lives, we might consider using it wisely, because God gave it to us freely. This brings us to the term "free will." Found only in the Old Testament, "freewill offerings" refer to voluntary contributions of animals for the atonement of sin or for the fulfillment of a vow. "Free will," simply put, is the freedom to make choices. There are no strings attached to our will, because God's expectations of us don't include strong-arming us into obedience. Yet, our freedom isn't without limitations. We aren't completely free from God's control, because the world is preserved and managed by him. Circumstances determine some of our choices, while our human nature motivates others. Therefore, decisions made of our own will and not restricted by outside forces are "free."

Think of the times we make decisions, knowing they aren't pleasing to God, yet still go forward. The consequences of such decisions, fueled by the power of sin, usually return to haunt us. We say, "I'll never do that again," and then suffer from the natural consequences and residual effects. Still, hope reigns supreme. As the pinnacle of creation, made free and therefore responsible for our actions, we have God's permission to adapt to his divine will, which results in the growth of our love relationship with him.

Remember, "It is for freedom that Christ has set us free. Stand firm, then, and do not let yourselves be burdened again by a yoke of slavery" (Gal. 5:1). We are released from the bondage of sin only through Christ's death on the cross. Still, authentic faith requires that we make a choice to follow Jesus. We can either exist in a love relationship with God or exclude him from our lives. It's a life or death, black or white decision. Trying to handle life with God part of the time and excluding him deliberately the rest of the time is dangerous.

Our Obedience Must Be Sacred and Secular

God's relational purpose between himself and us comes through covenants. God promises and we respond. In *Systematic Theology*, Wayne Grudem wrote that a covenant is an unchangeable, divinely imposed legal agreement between God and man that stipulates the conditions of their relationship. One such covenant is the covenant of grace.

We know from biblical history that we cannot conquer our sin. We sin and then our relationship with God is estranged. But God provided another way for us. He established the covenant of grace, which begins with placing our faith alone in Christ's redeeming work. We don't earn our salvation, God gives it to us solely through faith.

Authentic faith trusts in Christ for salvation, depends on him instead of ourselves, and willingly repents of sin over our lifetime. We continue in the covenant of grace by obeying Christ, which then confirms that we are legitimate believers and members of the new covenant.

We naturally thrust aside old behavioral patterns and embrace a new life when we commit our lives to Christ in authentic faith. Then our obedience leads us into the world and empowers us to devote ourselves to bringing others to faith in Jesus Christ.

Listen, our faith journey isn't about you and me, and it didn't just begin. By immersing ourselves in the biblical history of creation, the fall into sin, Israel's story, and the story of Jesus Christ we understand those earlier events so well that our lives are shaped and illuminated by Scripture. Feeling it in our bones, we look forward to Christ's return, and our obedience becomes second nature to us. Still, we face challenges.

For example, Paul defends himself against his critics in Corinth, who accused him of boldness from afar and meekness face-to-face:

> *I beg you that when I come I may not have to be as bold as I expect to be toward some people who think that we live by the standards of this world. For though we live in the world, we do not wage war as the world does. The weapons we fight with are not the weapons of the world. On the contrary, they have divine power to demolish strongholds. We demolish arguments and every pretension that sets itself up against the knowledge of God, and we take captive every thought to make it obedient to Christ. And we will be ready to punish every act of disobedience, once your obedience is complete* (2 Cor. 10:2–6).

Paul, whose authority was above reproach, looked at the obedience and disobedience of the Corinthians charitably, but also realistically. He knew that some in Corinth would fail. You and I fail. We are all disobedient. However, a perfect life isn't a requirement for authentic faith, and our obedience is a natural response that develops as we grow in our faith. That's not to say it's easy. When I am near failing but resist temptation, once the lure subsides, I feel satisfaction and peace.

Lastly, authentic obedience is sacred because it shows respect for the Living God. It is also secular because the unbelieving world sees God in us. If it were only one or the other, the world wouldn't notice that we are different. Ignoring the world's problems, we'd sit back and wait for heaven. The "let's wait and see" attitude is contrary to Christ's teachings. Accordingly, we should resist the temptation to sequester ourselves away from the world. The best response is to show our faith, and by showing our faith, inspire others. To paraphrase C. S. Lewis in *Mere Christianity*, "Do we want to be nice men and women; or do we want to be changed men and women?"

In Our Worst Moments, When We've Turned Away from God, We Persevere

As Paul explained, a constant battle rages in our soul. But what about the times when things are going smoothly, and we feel safe in the arms of God, never imagining that our faith would be tested due to our deliberate disobedience. What then?

David was a successful king, and during his reign Israel prospered. The Israelites defeated their enemies, brought the Ark of the Covenant to Jerusalem, and all in the Davidic kingdom was as it should have been. Just like David, all of us at one time have felt that our kingdom was as it should be. Now, try to place yourself on David's rooftop, overlooking your kingdom. You can't help but notice a beautiful woman bathing just below your vantage point. With no battles to fight, no wars to win, and nothing left to do, boredom has set in. She is so beautiful, what harm is there? No one can see you. And the rest is history. This biblical drama is a remarkable example of how our unburdened lives can turn on a dime. David and Bathsheba's tryst on the rooftop brought turmoil and tragedy to their lives. She became pregnant, David ordered her husband, Uriah, killed, and Nathan the prophet rebuked David.

> "[. . .] *This is what the* LORD, *the God of Israel, says:* '*I anointed you king over Israel, and I delivered you from the hand of Saul*'" (2 Sam. 12:7).
> "'*Now, therefore, the sword will never depart from your house, because you despised me and took the wife of Uriah the Hittite to be your own*'" (2 Sam. 12:10).

"But because by doing this you have shown utter contempt for the Lord, the son born to you will die" (2 Sam. 12:14).

Yet, David was "a man after [God's] own heart" (1 Samuel 13:14). The child died. David repented. He persevered.

Against you, you only, have I sinned and done what is evil in your sight; so you are right in your verdict and justified when you judge. [. . .] Create in me a pure heart, O God, and renew a steadfast spirit within me. Do not cast me from your presence or take your Holy Spirit from me. Restore to me the joy of your salvation and grant me a willing spirit, to sustain me. Then I will teach transgressors your ways, so that sinners will turn back to you (Ps. 51:4,10–13).

Like David in our worst moments, when we turn away from God, we must not give up. When our sin has run amok, we most need to drag ourselves out of the scum of who we are, and turn to the Lord. God listens, restores, and holds us, even though we don't deserve it. And once the relationship is resurrected in our heart, mercy, grace, peace, and joy fill us and we press on.

Mary Magdalene, a woman in the New Testament, endured and stood firm. We know that she suffered from a gloomy past, perhaps darkened by some form of mental illness. Despite her tormented early life, Mary never turned away from God. Interestingly, Mark's gospel tells us:

It was early on Sunday morning when Jesus came back to life, and the first person who saw him was Mary Magdalene—the woman from whom he had cast out seven demons (Mark 16:9, TLB).

Try to imagine Satan tormenting you with seven demons. You're wretched, melancholy, destitute, pitiful, and considered a pariah. Your victimized life, ruined beyond repair, is just like Mary Magdalene's life. Yet, Scripture doesn't dwell on her plight as a demon-possessed woman. Luke's gospel says this about her:

After this, Jesus traveled about from one town and village to another, proclaiming the good news of the kingdom of God. The Twelve were with him, and also some women who had been cured of evil spirits and diseases: Mary (called Magdalene) from whom seven demons had come out [. . .] (Luke 8:1–2).

Jesus healed Mary Magdalene by taking the seven demons from her. After this, Mary used her freedom, her resources, and her time to follow Jesus. Mary belonged to Jesus' inner circle and traveled with him throughout the rest of his life on earth. After the crucifixion and distraught over discovering an empty tomb, Mary remained intent on finding Jesus' dead body. When Jesus appeared to her, she didn't recognize him. We read, "Jesus said to her, 'Mary.' She turned toward him and cried out in Aramaic, 'Rabboni!' (which means 'Teacher')" (John 20:16). In *Twelve Extraordinary Women*, John MacArthur wrote, "Mary remained Jesus' faithful disciple even when others forsook him. She ended up loyally following him to the cross, and even beyond." What about us? Will we follow Jesus to the cross? Will we, like Mary Magdalene, be so intent on pursuing our faith that we cast aside all fear and surrender to him?

Reflection Questions

1. What does encountering your own "inner self" or "inner dimension" mean to you?

2. How do you think God is preparing a way for us?

3. Tell what you think it means that our heart is the seat of emotions, affections, intellect, and will. Explain a time when you made a bad decision and it came back to haunt you.

4. What does it mean that our obedience must be sacred and secular?

5. What did you learn from hearing David's response to his sin with Bathsheba?

CHAPTER SEVEN

God Rescues Us from Ourselves

The thief had nails through both hands, so that he could not work; and a nail through each foot, so that he could not run errands for the Lord; he could not lift a hand or a foot toward his salvation, and yet Christ offered him the gift of God; and he took it. Christ threw him a passport, and took him into Paradise.

– D. L. Moody

WITHOUT THE GOD-MAN, Jesus Christ, the Christian has no faith. Christ's persona, though somewhat eccentric, radical, and paradoxical, is the epitome of a best friend. The essence of Christ's incarnation into the God-man appears in Philippians 2:6–8:

Who, being in very nature God, did not consider equality with God something to be used to his own advantage; rather, he made himself nothing by taking the very nature of a servant, being made in human likeness. And being found in appearance as a man, he humbled himself by becoming obedient to death— even death on a cross!

Jesus Christ, the most dominant, powerful, and influential entity in the universe set aside his divine rights and glory to become a human being. He took on our human nature, lived with human limitations, felt our emotions and the perils of our existence, died on the cross for our sin, and suffered the agonizing pain of crucifixion. So, as we marvel at Jesus, the God-man, let's remind ourselves of why he came.

Destruction is Our Destiny Apart from Jesus Christ

Love, mercy, grace, and patience are the foundation of God's benevolence toward us, even in our wickedness. Isaiah explains the depth of our depravity:

All of us have become like one who is unclean, and all our righteous acts are like filthy rags; we all shrivel up like a leaf, and like the wind our sins sweep us away. No one calls on your name or strives to lay hold of you; for you have hidden your face from us and have given us over to our sins (Isa. 64:6–7).

We can't take Isaiah's words lightly, nor think they only apply to others. Like the fellow Jews of his day, Isaiah is describing you, me, and every other human being. Furthermore, the word choices Isaiah used grab our attention, for when translated from the Hebrew their meaning shows our sinfulness as seen through the eyes of God. For example, the unclean refers to lepers, and the filthy rags refer to menstrual rags.

Time Out

How can I possibly be as sinful as Isaiah described? When viewing ourselves through human eyes, rather than God's eyes, sin becomes less of an absolute. But we are all sinners and because God is perfect in every way, he cannot tolerate sin, so his view of sin is completely different from ours.

Isaiah spoke from experience. When God called him to be a prophetic voice, he suffered a moment of self-awareness about his sin, captured in the following passage.

In the year that King Uzziah died, I saw the Lord, high and exalted, seated on a throne; and the train of his robe filled the temple. Above him were seraphim, each with six wings: With two wings they covered their faces, with two they covered their feet, and with two they were flying. And they were calling to one another: "Holy, holy, holy is the LORD Almighty; the whole earth is full of his glory."

*At the sound of their voices the doorposts and
thresholds shook and the temple was filled with
smoke.*

*"Woe to me!" I cried. "I am ruined! For I am a
man of unclean lips, and I live among a people of
unclean lips, and my eyes have seen the King, the
LORD Almighty."*

*Then one of the seraphim flew to me with a live coal
in his hand, which he had taken with tongs from
the altar. With it he touched my mouth and said,
"See, this has touched your lips; your guilt is taken
away and your sin atoned for."*

*Then I heard the voice of the Lord saying, "Whom
shall I send? And who will go for us?"*

And I said, "Here am I. Send me!" (Isa. 6:1–8).

God called Isaiah, and in that moment, Isaiah
understood the depth of his sinfulness. Yet when the
seraphim placed the burning coal on Isaiah's lips, God
provided a way to cleanse and forgive Isaiah.

These Scriptures clearly show us the depth of our sin,
which separates us from God and causes spiritual death.
Just as physical death separates the spirit from the body,
spiritual death occurs when our sin separates us from God.
Furthermore, destruction is our destiny apart from Jesus
Christ, who serves as a mediator between God and us.

How do we apply Isaiah's experience to our lives?
When you have wronged someone, do they come to

you and say, "I forgive you," even though you haven't apologized? Possibly. Normally you call, text, or meet with them and say you're sorry. Sometimes people apologize through their actions. For example, after my dad mistreated my husband in a business situation and didn't speak to him for several years, he didn't apologize. Guilt overflowed, and he once told my Uncle Russ and Aunt Izzy, "God will never forgive me for all the things I've done."

But twenty years later, he custom built a section in our store. Despite suffering from congestive heart failure, he worked every day for a couple of hours in the morning, went home to rest, and then came back to work in the afternoon. A proud and successful businessman, I'm not sure apologies were a part of his DNA. And although I would have enjoyed seeing these two important men in my life reconciled earlier, his actions spoke volumes about how sorry he felt. Still, my dad suffered from guilt during most of his adult life.

Time Out

What does it mean to be truly sorry? If you genuinely feel sorry for your actions and the harm they've caused, you resolve to never repeat that action. It's hard to reject certain habitual actions, and we may need to be truly sorry more than once before we say no to the habit that hurt others forever. Sometimes, just saying no isn't as easy as it sounds.

Confessing and receiving God's forgiveness makes us healthier. The apostle John says, "If we confess our sins, he is faithful and just and will forgive us our sins and purify us from all unrighteousness" (1 John 1:9). John doesn't say, "if we sin." Instead, knowing that sin persistently clings to us, he acknowledges our sin. Some of us, on the other hand, say we have no sin. Nothing is further from the truth. The apostle John, in his first letter to believers, wrote:

> *This is the message we have heard from him and declare to you: God is light; in him there is no darkness at all. If we claim to have fellowship with him and yet walk in the darkness, we lie and do not live out the truth. But if we walk in the light, as he is in the light, we have fellowship with one another, and the blood of Jesus, his Son, purifies us from all sin. If we claim to be without sin, we deceive ourselves and the truth is not in us* (1 John 1:5–8).

Accordingly, God's justice, forgiveness, and purification depend on our acknowledgement of sin and our belief that Christ paid the price for it.

Since we all have fallen short of God's perfection, it's important to humble ourselves and recognize our sinfulness. In reverent respect for God, we repent, meaning that we turn away from our sins, one by one. Imagine that your spouse says, "I hate you" in a fit of anger. Would it be enough for him or her to say, "I'm sorry I was mean to you"? Wouldn't you rather hear, "I'm sorry I said, 'I hate you', because I don't hate you, I spoke out of anger, and I love you"?

Specificity in repentance makes us aware of exactly what our sins are, and shows God that we are prepared to make changes. God honors our repentance, he forgives us, accepts us, and loves us, far more than we can imagine. Paul wrote:

And I pray that you, being rooted and established in love, may have power, together with all the Lord's holy people, to grasp how wide and long and high and deep is the love of Christ, and to know this love that surpasses knowledge—that you may be filled to the measure of all the fullness of God. (Eph. 3:17–19).

> ### Time Out
>
> What does it mean to truly forgive? Although it's important to say, "I forgive you" when someone has hurt us, it's not enough. We may begrudge the person internally and carry unresolved anger. The person hurt the most by this is us. A life of bitterness ensues, and we suffer. It is important to process the incident fully over time, sometimes multiple times, so we can actually make a choice to forgive and let God take care of us through his mercy and grace.

Paul's prayer describes God's love as more than knowledge. He explains that only when we are rooted and established in love with all who love Jesus can we appreciate the fullness of God's love.

So, how do we sinners, living in the presence of God, keep from sinning? We don't; we concentrate on allowing Christ to live through us. We change our ways. We give up our old self, take on our new self, and submit ourselves to him. This is a complex and difficult concept for all of us, because submission implies power, control, and rule on the part of someone other than ourselves.

Submission to God takes us beyond ourselves and blesses us. As sinners, when we give ourselves up to God, we begin a new path that creates in us the holiness we subconsciously crave. It gives us freedom to flow into the shape God originally designed for us. The old self depletes itself, and the new self grows into God's intended mold. Eventually our daily surrender becomes the most, not the least, and we live surrounded by God's love and peace.

Even though God created us in his perfect image, Paul explains, "All have sinned and fall short of the glory of God, and all are *justified freely* by his grace through the redemption that came by Christ Jesus" (Rom. 3:23–24, emphasis added). Accordingly, as God dispenses his love, mercy, grace, and patience, Christ (our advocate) settles our debt, which brings reconciliation, redemption, return, and repentance.

Salvation Includes Rescue, Renewal, and Restoration

Many Christians talk about the "free gift of salvation." You may wonder, "But aren't all gifts free?" Well yes, and . . . no. Many of the gifts that people give aren't free. Perhaps the giver's motivation is to receive something in return, such as a large monetary "gift" during a political campaign, to impress someone, or cause the receiver to feel indebted to the giver.

However, the gift of salvation is given to us with no such strings attached, so God has truly given us the free gift of salvation.

Before we delve into the free gift of salvation, let's journey back to the sixteenth century and the movement known as the Protestant Reformation. As Justin Holcomb points out, Martin Luther and John Calvin were two of the visionaries that "spearheaded a movement that transformed Christianity and eventually led to the emergence of the Protestant denominations that exist today." In his article, "The Five Solas - Points from the Past that Should Matter to You," Holcomb reviews "The Five Solas [which] are five Latin phrases (or slogans) that emerged during the Reformation to summarize the Reformers' theological convictions about the essentials of Christianity."

The Five Solas are:

Sola Scriptura ("Scripture alone"): The Bible alone is our highest authority.

Sola Fide ("faith alone"): We are saved through faith alone in Jesus Christ.

Sola Gratia ("grace alone"): We are saved by the grace of God alone.

Solus Christus ("Christ alone"): Jesus Christ alone is our Lord, Savior, and King.

Soli Deo Gloria ("to the glory of God alone"): We live for the glory of God alone.

All God requires is that we place our faith in Christ alone (*Sola Christus*). Remember from chapter six that authentic faith makes us strong. Our hope for the future never fails, because we are confident, unafraid, and believe in God's promises. True faith is an eternal love relationship with God that makes us whole in mind, body, and spirit. And because we love God above all others, our life is full of him. Our response to this mystical, life-altering adventure builds over time until it occurs naturally, like breathing. This explanation of authentic faith is the epitome of placing our faith in Christ alone (*Sola Christus*).

With faith at the forefront of our mind, let's consider the word, "salvation." The meaning of salvation can refer to deliverance from ordinary dangers and conditions. But in a biblical sense, it refers to the protection of believers from righteous wrath in their relationship with God.

However, the shortest and most specific definition is the rescue of believers from sin and death.

Salvation isn't the end; it's the beginning. Once saved, God leads us into a life that is pleasing to him. The apostle Paul adds urgency to the situation, when he says, "And do this, understanding the present time: The hour has already come for you to wake up from your slumber, because our salvation is nearer now than when we first believed" (Rom. 13:11). He also said, "for you know very well that the day of the Lord will come like a thief in the night." (1 Thess. 5:2). Paul is motivating us to take action through his use of metaphorical phrases "wake up from your slumber", "understanding the present time", and "a thief in the night".

Lastly, in his *Book of Bible Lists*, H. L. Willmington shares four biblical truths we should remember when reflecting on the free gift of salvation:

Salvation is always by innocent blood (Heb. 9:22)

Salvation is always through a person [Jesus Christ] (Jonah 2:9; Acts 4:12; 1 Thess. 5:9; Heb. 5:9)

Salvation is always by grace (Eph. 2:8–9; Titus 2:11)

Salvation is always through faith (Rom. 5:1; Heb. 11:6)

Each of these four truths build upon the previous one and deserve a more in-depth explanation. When Willmington says "salvation is always by innocent blood," he is drawing a parallel from sacrifices described in the Old Testament (Lev. 4:32). Just as God required an unblemished lamb's innocent blood to atone for sin, through the new covenant, Jesus serves as the unblemished lamb, spilling his own blood to atone for our sins. Likewise, when Willmington says salvation is always through a person, he is, of course, referring to Christ (*Sola Fide*). An unblemished lamb was no longer enough; Jesus became the sacrifice. The third point is salvation is always by grace (*Sola Gratia*).[8] Now that God has made a path to salvation available through Christ, we cannot earn our salvation; it is through God's grace. And the last point salvation is always through faith (*Sola Fide*) refers to receiving the grace of God only through faith.

Responding to God's Compassion and Comfort Has Nothing to do With Religion

In the Christian faith, we rely on and believe in a personal God, along with the historical facts surrounding the birth, ministry, death, and resurrection of Jesus Christ. The New Testament book of Hebrews reminds us of Christ's sovereignty and adequacy. He is all we need. In chapter two, we saw Jesus as our High Priest enter the Most Holy Place, once and for all, by bleeding on the cross during his crucifixion, thus obtaining eternal redemption. In addition, Hebrews 10:19–23 says:

> *Therefore, brothers and sisters, since we have confidence to enter the Most Holy Place by the blood of Jesus, by a new and living way opened for us through the curtain, that is, his body, and since we have a great priest over the house of God, let us draw near to God with a sincere heart and with the full assurance that faith brings, having our hearts sprinkled to cleanse us from a guilty conscience and having our bodies washed with pure water. Let us hold unswervingly to the hope we profess, for he who promised is faithful.*

In this passage, we see the phrase "full assurance." This phrase, in the context of Christian faith, doesn't mean "maybe" or "perhaps." It means there is absolutely no doubt that we can enter into his presence, enjoy living in his light, add to his light through our witness, converse with him, love him, and be received by him, cleansed, consecrated, and prepared to approach him on the last day. This full assurance also protects us from Satan. Since God was willing to live amongst us in the flesh and die for us, let's not be suspicious or a skeptical.

The four phrases in Hebrews 10:19–23 are essential components in drawing near to God:

"Sincere heart" – without deception; genuine, true, and right

"Full assurance" – no doubting as to God's acceptance of us

"Hearts sprinkled" – the blood of Jesus that cleanses us from all guilt

"Our bodies washed" – with pure water; clean, innocent, and clear

The historical facts found in the Bible and authenticated by archeological discoveries surrounding the birth, ministry, death, and resurrection of Jesus Christ, declare that he is God. Yet those of us who don't read the Bible can't begin to fathom why Christians know what will happen to them after they die. Jesus' resurrection gives us hope in this life and the assurance of God accepting us in the life to come. It is through faith in him alone that we receive every ultimate and eternal blessing, which flows directly from God's grace.

We read in Psalm 27:3, "Though an army besiege me, my heart will not fear; though war break out against me, even then I will be confident." In the context of this verse, David, who was at war, spoke of his confidence, and his assurance of God's grace to deliver him. But "though an army besiege me" isn't always about war. To be sure, some

Christians today die for their faith, such as the beheadings of Middle Eastern Christians by ISIS. Other tribulations aren't so dramatic. It could be as simple as having a Facebook post censored because of religious content (which happened to me). We can look at certain events, attitudes, conversations, and mental attacks directed against us as our enemies, because they are antagonistic to God. They are all tribulations of life, and we cannot escape them. Contrary to what some believe, having a relationship with God does not remove adversity from our lives. In John 16:33 Jesus tells us, "[. . .] In this world you will have trouble. But take heart! I have overcome the world." Paul wrote:

> *Praise be to the God and Father of our Lord Jesus Christ, the Father of compassion and the God of all comfort, who comforts us in all our troubles, so that we can comfort those in any trouble with the comfort we ourselves receive from God* (2 Cor. 1:3–4).

Notice that we respond to God's mercies and comfort by comforting others who are in need, employing the bounty of comfort given to us. Hence, responding to God's compassion and comfort has nothing to do with religion, in the sense of rules, rituals, and restrictions. It's about a love relationship that surpasses all others. Through the overflow of his mercy and comfort toward us, we carry it forward. A collaboration occurs, in which God shows us mercy, and we respond by sharing it with others.

God unlocked the most Holy Place in heaven for us. Therefore, we can commune with him when our need is most desperate and for any length of time. As Jesus made it permissible for us to enter the Holy of Holies through his spilled blood on the cross, he is also fulfilling the requirements of the Law.

We Unknowingly Waste the Fruit of His Son's Sacrificial Act

We need salvation. Otherwise, we face uncertainty in life, death, and every event, crisis, or challenge in between. God has removed the uncertainties of life on our behalf so that we can rely on his sustaining authority in the world around us. But when we try to achieve salvation on our own, we disrupt and depreciate his free gift of salvation and unknowingly waste the fruit of his Son's sacrificial act of dying for us. Biblical history shows that our original destiny, to bear the image of an uncreated God (see Genesis 1:26–27), ceased to exist after the Garden of Eden. Yet God, in his love, mercy, and grace, sent his one and only Son to bear our sins. Jesus experienced ridicule, torture, excruciating pain, and crucifixion, the most agonizing way to die. Some may say, "Well Jesus knew his death wasn't permanent and that he would come back to life, so what's the big deal?"

Hearing this shortsighted statement made by a Christian during an adult Sunday school class made me sad. Still, it's an accurate example of innocence generated by disregard for the Word of God. Yes, Jesus knew he would rise again to sit at the right hand of the Father. But at the moment of his death, he felt the unbearable pain of being separated from his Father. In Mark 15:34, we read that after suffering most of the day, when he could bear no more, "And at three in the afternoon Jesus cried out in a loud voice [. . .] 'My God, My God, why have you forsaken me?'" Jesus' physical suffering of estrangement from the Father mirrors the pain of destruction, departure, and divorce we will feel if we remain separated from God at our death. Salvation is ours for the taking. And the decision is ours alone.

Reflection Questions

1. What is your understanding of sin causing spiritual death and how does it coincide with physical death?

2. How did you feel when you read about Isaiah's call and the way God dealt with Isaiah's sin?

3. When was the last time you needed rescue, renewal, and restoration? What happened and how did you feel?

4. What do you think about the idea that responding to God's compassion and comfort has nothing to do with religion?

5. How would you respond to the four components (sincere heart, full assurance, hearts sprinkled, our bodies washed) that bring us closer to God? (Hebrews 10:22)

6. What does human effort to gain salvation look like and do you think it is time well spent?

PART IV

LIVING NEAR TO GOD

Nearness to God brings likeness to God.
The more you see God the more of God will be seen in you.

– Charles H. Spurgeon

CHAPTER EIGHT

An Ordered Life

One bold message in the Book of Job is that you can say anything to God. Throw at him your grief, your anger, your doubt, your bitterness, your betrayal, your disappointment—he can absorb them all. As often as not, spiritual giants of the Bible are shown contending with God. They prefer to go away limping, like Jacob, rather than to shut God out [. . .]

– Philip Yancey

MAINTAINING AN ORDERED life isn't about list-making, scheduling, rigidity, or always being on time. It's about knowing who we are, prioritizing the entanglements people bring to our lives, and establishing new life patterns that bring us joy and contentment. People order their lives differently. As Secularism takes some of our hearts, we ignore our deepest longings, and live only in the extraneous world of performance and productivity.

Today's culture frowns upon the practice of listening to our hearts. Instead, we are encouraged to seek beauty, wealth, intelligence, and acceptance. But what if your heart stopped beating and you felt your life ebbing away?

Our True Stories Are Not What People See

The people who've divorced themselves from the heartbeats of life may feel themselves disintegrating before their very eyes. They aren't aware, until it's too late. The episodes I've mentioned in my dad's life clearly demonstrate his inability to listen to his heart. When he finally listened, it was too late for him to live guilt-free, because he was near death. Dad lived his life story externally. And although we didn't get to see his internal story, it was there. Sometimes we replace a loving God relationship with working for God activity, living only in our external story.

The point is that our true stories are not what people see. They are the journeys of our inner hearts. In *The Sacred Romance*, the late Brent Curtis and John Eldredge wrote, "Jesus himself knew that if people lived only in the outer story, eventually they would lose track of their inner life, the life of their heart he so much desired to redeem." Thus, ordering our lives begins with our hearts.

Remembering our universal and personal history helps us prepare an ordered life. It's also a good idea to examine our personal evolution as children of God, our personality traits, and particular temperament. Since God knows everything about us, it helps if we agree with his assessments. Looking at our life as a calling from God gives it cosmic importance.

The Good We Accomplish in Our Lifetime Answers a Call from God

Whether we know it or not, we all receive a general call on our lives that comes from God. It's an invitation to follow him. The proposal (God's plan for our life) began at creation and lasts for eternity. We decide whether to answer the call. Some people may ask, "But doesn't God just call people who devote their lives to church work, such as a pastor?" No, God may call us in a specific way that has nothing to do with church, or to an immediate problem, such as caring for a loved one. Specific calls, such as accounting, nursing, playing the saxophone, writing poetry, or teaching are unique and apply to our jobs, talents, and aspirations. They give us purpose, a reason for being, and can change over our lifetime.

Time Out

How do I recognize God's call on my life? When you are doing something that's really hard, makes an impact, and you love doing it, that's what God has called you to do. God's calls are different, because they intertwine with the way that God has specifically created the individual, as we grow more mature in our faith, or when life circumstances change.

For example, a young person's career in the medical field is gratifying, but once they become a parent, they may decide to stay at home until the children are older. On the other hand, if a loved one becomes disabled or is very sick, we might need to rearrange our life in order to care for them. These particular examples answer a call from God. The three expressions of our calling (general, specific, and immediate) work together as we respond to God and approach the world around us.

Thus, the finest order for our life fits our talents, longings, and hearts. It causes us to flourish. It gives us a reason for greeting each day with joy. We receive fulfillment in our lives when we align ourselves with our God-given inclinations: our personality, gifts, talents, and aptitudes. Most important, we have the freedom to be who we are and what God meant us to be. We live freely within the context of our purposed life, and manage ourselves accordingly. Rather than living helter-skelter, haphazardly, and full of angst, we prioritize our lives. We put "first things first." And the first thing is our relationship with God.

An Ordered Life Involves Doing Things Differently

When the empty nest years of marriage began, my husband and I focused on each other and ourselves. Individual pride caused arguments in our business. We each accepted God's call to follow him, but failed miserably. We had put our business life, limited social life, and church life in conflicting spaces. We eventually agreed to eliminate the competition for our souls and put everything, all of our lives, under God.

Imagine that you are filling a vase with decorative stones to keep a single long stem rose in place before putting the water in. After filling the vase with water, you try to shove the rose stem into the stones, but the stem breaks. But if you put the rose into the vase, hold it steady, and then carefully put the stones in around it, the rose will stand upright, ready for the water. It's the same in life, there is an order to things that surpasses all others.

Once my husband and I placed God into the center of our marriage, we could easily fit the rest in. Every morning we sat down and read Scripture or a faith-based book together. Our reading time often lasted only a few minutes, but our

Time Out

How do I intentionally order my life? Identify your core beliefs; what would you want someone to say at your funeral? The way they describe you shows what was important to you.

By translating your core belief in God into concrete action, such as participating in a ministry at your church, or keeping imperishable food in your car to give to the homeless, your life goals take on a new meaning.

Begin every day with gratitude, and feed your soul with Christian music, for example, on your way to work or during your daily walk. When you get off track, stay calm, don't feel guilty, and get back to it as soon as possible.

morning ritual morphed into an intentionally ordered life.

It's important to realize we can't do everything. Sometimes we need to say no. We try to do more than we should, perhaps out of a need for recognition or still trying to earn our salvation. Paul wrote to the Colossians, "For though I am absent from you in body, I am present with you in spirit and delight to see how disciplined you are and how firm your faith in Christ is" (Col. 2:5). Just as Paul encouraged the Colossians, Jesus is with us in spirit. He delights in our orderly ways. We can say no. We don't have to do more for recognition. Our acceptance into God's family is far more important than receiving approval from people. God rescues us from ourselves, gives us self-discipline, we learn to say no, and we inhabit our uniquely ordered life.

Sometimes We Need to Break Away from Community

Living in community with others, Christian or not, enhances our lives. We converse, learn from each other, and help one another during difficult times. Nevertheless, only spending our time in mutual connection with a specific community can sometimes feel restrictive because of our inability to meet everyone's expectations and conform to group behavior and culture. For example, we might subconsciously mimic group members regarding clothing or hairstyles, or feel pressured to make lifestyle choices that aren't compatible with ours. Making these choices feels uncomfortable, so it's important to occasionally break away from one of our communities to figure out why we caved to their influences. In our struggle to understand the impulses of others and ourselves, we feel annoyed. Therefore, we sometimes need solitude.

I've tried to re-join my women's Bible study group twice since graduating from college, and both times I realized I shouldn't be there. Focused on my writing (both times), I found myself itching to leave early. I hadn't done the homework nor studied the Scriptures ahead of time, because I wanted to be home, alone in my study, at my computer, writing my book. Since I had previously loved Bible study, this troubled me. In this instance, I needed solitude to discern why, suddenly, the women's Bible study wasn't a priority. After thinking about it, it finally dawned on me that finishing my book should be the higher priority, but only at that particular time.

Solitude isn't always spent in prayer or meditation. For example, I use my alone time to reflect on my life, like why I'm emotionally up and down at times, where to find grace for people who have disappointed me, and how to accept my limitations as I age. It's also the time for doing my best work, because I'm comfortable and aware of my purpose to finish this book. This doesn't mean my priorities change in terms of caring for my husband, relating with my children and grandchildren, or not helping a friend in their time of need. For others, solitude may include journaling, a daily essay where they write about their inner thoughts, a narrative of prayer, or an encounter with God.

In *Courage and Calling*, Gordon T. Smith wrote, "When we are people who live in community, solitude is the critical spiritual discipline that enables us to draw on the strengths of the conversation we have in community while avoiding the ways in which community is oppressive." Without solitude, the needs of others might consume us. Let's remember that although we're made in God's image and he shares some of his attributes with us, we shouldn't expect to perform like him. Most important, the lack of balance between solitude and community inadvertently restricts the flow of God's work of sanctification (changing us).

Think about trying to spend time only in solitude. There wouldn't be points of reference to ponder, because we wouldn't have the discussions with other people to think about. Sometimes we think we need solitude more than we do. We may feel pressured to escape from people and/ or stress brought on by life and work. However, spending too much time in solitude can lead to self-centeredness and potential depression. If we don't commune with other people, we don't learn new things, hear about other people's lives, or spend time evaluating the world around us.

The Sanctification Process Has No End
Another point in ordering our life relates to our past. And although we don't want to forget lessons learned,

there are times when we need to rid ourselves of guilt, shame, regrets, past failures, and/or relationships that hurt us. Time spent in confession, forgiveness of others, and self-awareness helps us do that. By dwelling too much on our past we allow Satan to manipulate us, making guilt and shame the focus of our lives instead of Christ. Some people refer to Satan's activity as arrows. Try to imagine that each point of each arrow has a memo attached, and when it pierces our hearts, the memo always boils down to two sentences found in the third chapter of Genesis: "Did God really say, 'You must not eat from any tree in the garden'?" (Gen. 3:1) and later, "'You will not certainly die,' the serpent said to the woman.'" (Gen. 3:4). If we truly believe what the Bible says, we can't refute the fact that Satan is alive and well in the twenty-first century. Still there is hope. God's provision against Satan's attacks comes from his act of sanctifying us. On the eve of his betrayal, Jesus prayed for our sanctification:

> *I have given them your word and the world has hated them, for they are not of the world any more than I am of the world. My prayer is not that you take them out of the world but that you protect them from the evil one. They are not of the world, even as I am not of it. Sanctify them by the truth; your word is truth* (John 17:14–17).

The sanctification process has no end. To explain sanctification, try to imagine a rose bush that's been unattended for many years. It languishes in unfertilized dirt; its branches aren't pruned. A few long branches reach up with a couple of buds, but the buds never bloom.

We are like that rose bush. God prunes us at every opportunity. The cutting hurts, but through it we begin growing into the likeness of Jesus. Jesus tells us:

"I am the true vine, and my Father is the gardener.
He cuts off every branch in me that bears no fruit,
while every branch that does bear fruit he prunes so
that it will be even more fruitful" (John 15:1–2).

God's pruning produces fruitfulness and "good fruit" represents godliness. God's work on our behalf continues until we take our last breath. Still, some people like me, don't always cooperate with God when he is conforming us to his original vision. The discovery that I had failed to cooperate with God came during a conversation with a former pastor.

"I haven't heard much about your conversion story," he said. "Tell me about it."

"Well, there were no cloud bursts and the sky didn't fall in," I replied. "It took a long time for my commitment to kick in—years, in fact."

"How much time passed before you took the relationship seriously?" asked the pastor.

"Oh my goodness—it took years and years." With tears streaming down my face, I asked, "Why do you think it took so long?"

"Well, I believe it took a very long time, because God had a lot of work to do in you."

That was a defining moment in my life, because I found the reason for my years of living as a half-baked Christian. I wasn't cooperating. I didn't pay enough attention to God. My focus lacked order. Business ambition, the desire to impress others, and absorption over how I looked were perched on the rungs of life's ladder above God.

James 3:16 is a perfect description of what happens in an unordered life: "For where you have envy and selfish ambition, there you find disorder and every evil practice." Envy, selfish ambition, and disorder come from Satan. On the other

Time Out

How do I get out of God's way so he can do his work in me? This is difficult, because we want to "help" God, but he doesn't really need our assistance in changing us to who he first imagined us to be. So, we submit, resubmit, and submit again to his authority over our lives. I know, we dislike authority, but believe me, submitting to God takes the chaos and brokenness out of our lives, so we can live in beautiful ways.

hand, when we live a properly ordered life, our soul deepens and expands with the presence of God, and we live beyond the superficial strips of life that keep us enslaved to sin.

God Transforms Us

Our spirits will naturally move back and forth as the seasons of life change, just as the waves of the oceans need to ebb and flow. This movement, much like breathing, comes from certain spiritual disciplines that transport us to the throne of God for his transforming work. In *Celebration of Discipline: The Path to Spiritual Growth*, Richard Foster named his first chapter, "The Spiritual Disciplines: Door to Liberation."

There are three categories of spiritual disciplines: the inward, the outward, and the corporate. None is most important, nor are they reserved for the holiest, most spiritually mature, or theologically informed. Instead, they enhance the spiritual lives of anyone who seeks to grow in their faith. Walking diligently on the path of life, we learn that we change only by God's grace, and that although his grace is free, it is not cheap. So we become explorers and students, as God genuinely transforms us. The inward disciplines of meditation, prayer, fasting, and Bible study are antithetical to the world around us. Meditation (apart from yoga classes) and prayer aren't popular discussion topics. Regardless, meditation and prayer keep us in touch with God.

One of my most memorable encounters with God occurred when asked to serve as a deacon at my church. After filling out the application form, I felt overwhelmed with desperation.

"Jesus," I cried out. "I want to serve you in the worst way, but when the nominating committee reads this application they'll know everything about me. How can I be a deacon after they read my application? They won't want me." For the first time in my life, I felt the calming presence of Jesus. He was so close. I felt as if I could touch Him. At that moment, I heard Jesus speak inaudibly to me. He said, "You can serve as a Deacon, I've cleansed and forgiven you; I've taken away your shame." If I hadn't cried out in prayer, I wouldn't have experienced Jesus in such a personal way.

Fasting, or abstaining from food for spiritual reasons, is a spiritual discipline in several religions. While Jesus didn't command us to fast, it can help us regain control in our lives and keep us balanced. Still, in most cases, fasting is a personal matter between the individual and God.

Study, however, is the most favorable way to discern the truth of Scripture. It provides an objective foundation for meditation and prayer. Furthermore, it garners our attention and helps us focus on the structure and content of the different books of the Bible. More important, study teaches us about the reality of events and actions as they pertain to God's ordering of the universe.

The outward disciplines of simplicity, solitude, submission, and service are inward realities that govern our outward lifestyle. The four outward disciplines cause the people around us to desire what we have, a relationship with God. Simplicity increases our awareness of the condition of those around us, and enables us to be empathetic to their hardships. Submission to God's will brings us closer to living beautifully in the brokenness of our world, because we know God is at work despite what we see. Service provides opportunities to apply our faith in the daily circumstances we encounter. Certain opportunities for service exist in our church, school, workplace, and community, but for people committed to the discipline of service, opportunities might present themselves without prompting. Our job is to recognize them and take action, even when it's inconvenient.

The corporate disciplines of confession, worship, guidance, and celebration usually involve a community of believers. We corporately confess our sin during the sacrament of the Lords' Supper and worship God with praise and thanksgiving during Sunday worship services. We also corporately celebrate marriages, births, and even the death of loved ones whom we know are suffering no longer. Supporting one another through the tribulations of life, we pray for our fellow believers. James wrote:

Admit your faults to one another and pray for each other so that you may be healed. The earnest prayer of a righteous man has great power and wonderful results (James 5:16, TLB).

Taking Time Away from Daily Life Thwarts Satan

Jesus knew the power of Satan, which begs the question, "Then, why don't we take Satan seriously?" Unaware of the manipulations and misdeeds of Satan, we often don't recognize his arrows, because we are distracted and live in the clamor of busyness and cluttered thoughts. We aren't aware that Satan is the underlying influence when we feel unworthy, become suspicious of a friend, or face temptation to go against what we know is right. His schemes are undetectable when we live in disarray, with no palpable purpose, and without a sense of God's nearness.

Immediately after John baptized Jesus, the Holy Spirit led the God-man out into the desert. An interesting turn of events, wouldn't you agree? Why didn't the Holy Spirit

Time Out

How do I recognize Satan when he is at work in my life? This question goes back to letting the Holy Spirit be our conscience. Further, when we feel ourselves getting out of control or angry over things we can't clearly define, it's time to take a step back and figure out what's going on. Sometimes when I find myself thinking unhealthy thoughts, I speak aloud and say, "Get away from me, Satan!" And I feel he's left.

prompt Jesus to put on his sandals, hit the rocky trail, and get going? Because God chose to lead Jesus into temptation, to test Jesus, to demonstrate that even though Jesus was human, he could still resist Satan. Jesus spent forty days and nights in solitude while the devil constantly tried to trick him. But Jesus stood firm. In the same way, Jesus' last act of obedience caused him to suffer alone, in excruciating pain, his hands and feet driven into a wooden cross by rusty nails. Jesus' two examples of obedience are a mirror image of what it means to live beautifully in a broken world.

God prepares us to face the temptations of life through sanctification. And by following Jesus' example of taking time away from daily life, we find ourselves reflecting on the condition of our relationship with him. God has our back in all circumstances and reaches down to lift us up into our love relationship with him. As our focus on God becomes more profound and passionate, our lives stabilize and we confront Satan with confidence. All things fall into their appropriate places. Fitting ourselves into his plans, God guides us as we grow nearer to him.

Reflection Questions

1. How do you maintain order in your life?

2. Tell about the appropriate ways in which you bring your inner life out in the open. In what ways do you think self-awareness informs an ordered life?

3. What are different calls on your life?

4. What do you think is a good strategy for balancing community and solitude?

5. Tell about times when Satan had the upper hand in your life and how you responded to him. What are your observations?

CHAPTER NINE

A Witness

The two most important days in your life are the day you are born and the day you find out why.

– Mark Twain

THE THREE TEENAGERS in the back of the nine-passenger van I was driving through Eastern Europe gave me the nickname "Curbie." They gave me this nickname because every time I tried to turn a corner on the narrow, crowded streets in Budapest, Hungary, I invariably ran over a curb. As the sole leader of a three-week mission trip, several other interesting experiences were in store for me.

After spending several hours waiting to pass through the border crossing, I began driving on Romanian "highways" which were slightly terrorizing as I white knuckled the steering wheel and passed wagons loaded with vegetables and speeding cars over bridges and narrow roads. But nothing had prepared me for our first church service, three days in to our adventure. Upon arriving in Cluj, Romania, the host church asked me to give my testimony, right then and there.

Without any notes, I prayed silently, glanced up to God, and began to tell my story. After saying a couple of sentences, I stopped and waited for the interpreter, and then continued. Many women came rushing over to me after the service. Most were crying. Talking in broken English, they told me how touched they were to hear my story. That experience helped me realize that my life story could leave God's imprint on the hearts of the people who heard it.

What Would Happen if We Witnessed as Jesus Did?

Jesus witnessed through his actions and by telling stories; so can we. To witness about our faith is to tell our story, just as I did in Cluj, Romania.

Every story needs telling. They bear witness to the facts pointing to a risen Savior and our salvation. Sometimes telling our story is risky. The idea that everyone believes in Jesus and wants to hear your story isn't a foregone

Time Out

How do I tell my story without getting emotional or seeming self-absorbed? Why not be emotional? An emotional testimony breaks down barriers. It brings listeners to the very brink of their own misery and helps them relate to what you're saying. Not one person who listens to a true, heartfelt story about how God changed your life will think you're self-absorbed.

conclusion. Furthermore, we are constrained by laws, workplace policies, and a general disregard for biblical truth. Hence, the possibility of family misunderstandings, losing a job, or losing a friend due to our witness is real. However, if we choose to live safe, we lose opportunities to bring others to Christ. Hebrews 5:8 explains, "Son though he was, he learned obedience from what he suffered." Being Christ-like in the context of this verse means that we are willing to learn how to witness for Christ, even though we may suffer for it.

Witnessing about our faith may seem complicated, because we worry that we might forget a Scripture, which becomes a convenient excuse for why we don't want to be God's witness. How many times have we started to share our faith and then stopped because we were afraid to offend, cause an argument, or perhaps even lose a friend? In John 8:13–14 we read:

The Pharisees challenged him, "Here you are, appearing as your own witness; your testimony is not valid."

Jesus answered, "Even if I testify on my own behalf, my testimony is valid, for I know where I came from and where I am going. But you have no idea where I come from or where I am going" (John 8:13–14).

What would happen if we witnessed as Jesus did? We can. Our testimony is true. We know about our "before Jesus life" and our "after Jesus life." In this Scripture, Jesus gives the blueprint for sharing our testimony. Knowing where we came from and where we are going speaks volumes. We know we came into the world as a sinner, and we know we will live with Jesus forever in heaven.

Witnessing for Jesus is a completely different model of success than the worldly view of success, because it isn't measured by how many folks we convert to Christianity, or how eloquently we tell our story. Once we've proclaimed the good news of the gospel, God takes it from there and changes the hearts of those who want to be changed.

We Must Not be Ashamed to Speak the Word of God

If you struggle with doubts and fears about being a witness for God, you're not alone. However, sharing a life-changing experience or life-saving story with someone should come naturally, even though it's not as simple as telling someone you found a cure for cancer. But what if? What if you discovered a cure for cancer? Wouldn't you be shouting it out to the world? Why then wouldn't we want to share a new discovery that cures the sickness of sin and assures us of salvation and eternal life?

While Noah built an ark that measured the length of one and a half football fields and was the height of a four-story building, in the middle of a drought, miles away from any body of water, he probably heard some pretty interesting comments from bystanders. Perhaps laughing aloud, they couldn't believe their eyes. Still, Noah persevered.

Imagine the mocking memes, Twitter trolls, and nasty Facebook comments, insulting us when posting about our calling to witness for God. Would we persevere, as Noah did, under the pressure of today's social media environment? It's a question worth considering, because Noah, our example, faced tremendous peer pressure. When the floodwaters came upon the earth, Noah's act of obedience brought glory to God because, "Noah did everything just as God commanded him" (Gen. 6:22). Noah witnessed through his actions, actions that in today's world would bring ridicule. And yet, Noah persevered.

The Bible teaches us how to be a good witness. Showing others how you live is a good beginning:

> *Do everything readily and cheerfully—no bickering, no second-guessing allowed! Go out into the world uncorrupted, a breath of fresh air in this squalid and polluted society. Provide people with a glimpse of good living and of the living God. Carry the light-giving Message into the night so I'll have good cause to be proud of you on the day that Christ returns. You'll be living proof that I didn't go to all this work for nothing* (Phil. 2:14–16, MSG).

Paul is encouraging us to go out into the world, as broken as it is, and show others that because of our relationship with the Living God, we can live beautifully. We are witnesses to Christ's light. All we need do is compare the darkness of our "before Jesus" life to the light of our "after Jesus" life to tell others about this cosmic phenomenon, Furthermore, God Almighty stands with us and watches out for us.

Some People Won't Listen

After God chose Moses to lead the Israelites out of Egypt, Moses and Aaron addressed Pharaoh.

> *Afterward Moses and Aaron went to Pharaoh and said, "This is what the LORD, the God of Israel, says: 'Let my people go, so that they may hold a festival to me in the wilderness.'"*
>
> *Pharaoh said, "Who is the LORD, that I should obey him and let Israel go? I do not know the LORD and I will not let Israel go"* (Exod. 5:1–2).

In this passage, Pharaoh said he didn't know the Lord and therefore didn't need to obey. In today's world, we've all heard about Jesus. However, the people we are trying to reach may have heard about Jesus in some superficial way. That doesn't mean they believe in him or know him. If they did know him, well . . . there would be no reason to be a witness and the world we are living in wouldn't be chaotic and broken. The world needs Jesus, even though many people don't know it or won't admit it.

Jesus said, "As you sent me into the world, I have sent them into the world. For them I sanctify myself, that they too may be truly sanctified" (John 17:18–19). Christ calls us to collaborate with him in transforming the world, because just as the Father sent Jesus into the world, Jesus sends us. Jesus knew all about the corrupt conditions that will confront us, because they confronted him as well. Nevertheless, avoiding this broken world isn't an option. We must learn to engage in the world as it is, and live beautifully as God's light in the darkness.

When trying to teach toddlers how to tie their shoes, it usually takes some time for our efforts to pay off, and we often need to keep reminding them even after they know how. Witnessing is no different. In many instances when we think we've presented the gospel succinctly or told our story in ways that we think people can relate to, we may not see the desired response, and/or it may take longer than expected (or many reminders) for a positive response. Some people won't listen. Many will try to change the subject. When Jesus talked to the woman at the well, he dealt with this same problem.

He told her, "Go, call your husband and come back."
"I have no husband," she replied.

Jesus said to her, "You are right when you say you have no husband. The fact is, you have had five husbands, and the man you now have is not your husband. What you have just said is quite true."
"Sir," the woman said, "I can see that you are a prophet. Our ancestors worshiped on this mountain, but you Jews claim that the place where we must worship is in Jerusalem" (John 4:16–20)

Once the woman realized Jesus knew about her past, she changed the subject. A normal reaction, wouldn't you agree? We may want to hear the good news, but not when our past becomes part of the discussion. Why is this? Perhaps we don't want to be judged or worry about whether we'll pass muster when we seek God. Or maybe we aren't interested in changing our lifestyle. Interestingly, she believed, gave an account of what happened, and became a witness for Christ.

Then, leaving her water jar, the woman went back to the town and said to the people, "Come, see a man who told me everything I ever did. Could this be the Messiah?" They came out of the town and made their way toward him (John 4:28–30).

Our Task of Reconciliation
Many people during Jesus' time on earth didn't believe in him, even though they witnessed his miracles.

Some spent their entire lives rejecting Jesus, while others believed in him, but refused to admit it. Regardless, our main concern is to fulfill our mission, despite what people do or don't believe. It's so important to Jesus that we go out for him, that he repeats his call for us to become witnesses five times in Scripture, as paraphrased below:

> Make disciples of all nations, teaching them to obey all I have commanded you (Matt. 28:19–20).

> Go into all the world and preach the gospel to all creation (Mark 16:15).

> Repentance for the forgiveness of sins will be preached in his name to all nations (Luke 24:47).

> As the Father has sent me, I am sending you (John 20:21).

> You will receive power when the Holy Spirit comes on you; and you will be my witnesses (Acts 1:8).

Jesus is calling us to be his witness. We have an opportunity to share our story about when, where, and why we gave ourselves to him. Still, there is the question of, "How?" You'll notice a few key words in the above

Scriptures: teach, preach, send, go, and be witnesses. Most of us are not teachers or preachers, but we can still go and be witnesses. Let's not forget, we have the power of the Holy Spirit living within us, and we can witness in different ways.

We can share our story over a cup of coffee with a friend. We might mentor a teenager, help a neighbor in need, show patience at the grocery store, or while driving. We don't need to say anything to be the hands and feet of Jesus. In everyday life, there are countless opportunities to share our faith.

> **Time Out**
>
> How can I get past my fear and share the Word? Pray beforehand, if it's a planned testimony. If not, silently pray for one moment, saying something like, "God, anoint me. God, give me the words. Help me." Once you start telling your story, it flows naturally.

Therefore, if anyone is in Christ, the new creation has come: The old has gone, the new is here! All this is from God, who reconciled us to himself through Christ and gave us the ministry of reconciliation (2 Cor. 5:17–18).

Establish a Relationship with the Person First

The doorbell rang on a Sunday afternoon, and when I opened the door, four people were standing on my front porch. They looked familiar. When they introduced themselves, I knew they were from our church, and I invited them in. "If you died today, do you know if you would go to heaven?" one of them asked. Taken aback, I became flustered. We had recently returned to the United States after living in Seoul for three years and attended this new church three or four times. Immature in my beliefs, that question offended me. Now, as a mature Christian, it would still offend me. It was not the question, but the brazen, overbearing attitude that came with the question. If I had some sort of relationship with at least one of those people, I would react differently.

Witnessing about God's mercy, love, and grace, and how he has changed us isn't the same as asking probing questions about a person's faith. Witnessing is akin to storytelling, not passing judgment with a "holier than thou" attitude. We don't know the extent of a person's biblical knowledge, the details of their life, or where they are in their search for something greater than themselves. A kinder, gentler approach works best. In 1 Peter 3:15, we read:

> But in your hearts revere Christ as Lord. Always be
> prepared to give an answer to everyone who asks you
> to give the reason for the hope that you have. But do
> this with gentleness and respect.

We need to establish a relationship with the person beforehand. If we are witnessing to a homeless person, for example, we may feel inclined to tell them about Jesus, but our first priority is to assess their situation, which might be to give them food and offer to help them find shelter.

The Good Samaritan didn't ask the beaten man if he was saved before he helped him:

> "But a Samaritan, as he traveled, came where the man was; and when he saw him, he took pity on him. He went to him and bandaged his wounds, pouring on oil and wine. Then he put the man on his own donkey, brought him to an inn and took care of him. The next day he took out two denarii and gave them to the innkeeper. 'Look after him,' he said, 'and when I return, I will reimburse you for any extra expense you may have'" (Luke 10:33–35).

So how can we apply the parable of the Good Samaritan to the ways we witness? It may be as simple as sitting next to a stranger at a church service, and offering to take them to lunch. Show hospitality. Ask low-key questions. Be a good listener. Tell the truth and be authentic.

Remember, it's about Jesus, not us. Live a life that will make others notice you are different. Show love, mercy, and grace. Let the person think about what you've shared.

Some may have negative opinions about witnessing and evangelizing, but Scripture isn't negative about either one. Still, they are a bit different. Evangelizing is proclaiming the gospel message in a persuasive way, perhaps handing out salvation tracts at a homeless shelter, a bus stop, or street corner. When we witness, we attest to the truth of what God has done in our life. We aren't trying to persuade. We are hoping that the person will make a decision for Christ. We follow up and nurture our relationship with the person.

Of course, in today's social media environment, witnessing is even more difficult. It seems as though social media has become a platform for saying things we would never dream of saying to someone in person. And the results have been tragic. People have killed themselves at the prompting of others' posts or texts. Kindness and understanding go a long way. It's okay if someone doesn't listen. And be prepared. You might face backlash from people, even friends and family, when you witness. Don't take it personally. Maybe, they aren't ready to make a decision for Christ. Pray and continue to nurture your relationships.

Witnessing isn't a one-time encounter. There are times when many years later, a person receives Christ because of our witness and we never hear about it. In either case, whether witnessing or evangelizing, the Holy Spirit is leading. We cannot open a person's head and pour the gospel into their brains like a glass of orange juice. But God working through the Holy Spirit changes every heart that wants to change. And God honors every effort when we share the good news of Christ.

God's Ultimate Plans for Humanity

When we read, "Go into all the world and preach the gospel to all creation" in Mark 16:15, Jesus isn't just addressing the missionaries throughout the world. He is addressing us, and we should consider being a witness by our words and actions in the diverse culture where we live and when visiting foreign countries. Many of us find it much easier to travel overseas in our retirement years.

However, retiring from the workplace doesn't mean retiring from the great commission and the ministry of reconciliation. God's call to witness lasts a lifetime, until our dying day. And everything we do today, retired or not, is preparation for eternal life. The finality of God's purposes is beautifully portrayed in Revelation 5:9–10.

> *And they sang a new song, saying: "You are worthy to take the scroll and to open its seals, because you were slain, and with your blood you purchased for God persons from every tribe and language and people and nation. You have made them to be a kingdom and priests to serve our God, and they will reign on the earth"* (Rev. 5:9–10).

In this passage, we see God's ultimate plans for humanity brought to fruition. We don't observe anything about religion, rules, or rituals. What we notice are these things:

God's people from every tribe, language, and nation are singing a new song

They are praising Jesus because he purchased them with his blood

Jesus has made them to be a kingdom and priests to serve God

They will reign on the earth

Our faith life exists not for us, but for God. We belong to him and he is the One in whom all things are possible. There is no greater privilege than to tell the world about the saving grace that comes from a love relationship with the living God.

Reflection Questions

1. Describe a time when you started to witness and then changed your mind. Why did you change your mind?

2. What does it mean when we say, "Our testimony is true" (John 19:35)?

3. How does it help to know where we came from and where we are going?

4. Explain the phrase, "God working through the Holy Spirit changes every heart that wants to change."

5. How do you feel knowing that Jesus wants us to collaborate with him in transforming the world?

6. What do you think it means when we say that everything we do today is preparation for eternal life?

CHAPTER TEN

The Christ-Centered Worldview

Few people seem to realize that the resurrection of Jesus is the cornerstone to a worldview that provides the perspective to all of life.

– Josh McDowell

THE CULMINATION OF our discussions about faith lead us to worldview thinking. Just like any other compelling new word, "worldview" has begun to show signs of misuse and misinterpretation. For example, Del Tackett, president of the Focus Leadership Institute, in his article "What's Your View of the World?" wrote: "I have heard people use it [worldview] as a synonym for *personality*, as in 'She has such a delightful worldview.' You have undoubtedly heard it—maybe even used it. But do you know what it means?" Sigmund Freud wrote:

By Weltanschauung [worldview], *then, I mean an intellectual construction which gives a unified solution of all the problems of our existence in virtue of a comprehensive hypothesis, a construction, therefore, in which no question is left open and in which everything in which we are interested finds a place.*

Freud's worldview is scientism, a system of schemes that don't relate to real life, so it isn't a practical model for a worldview. Real life leaves us with unanswered questions, lack of uniformity, unsolved problems, and no fixed places. Therefore, to uncover a worldview that actually works for us, we need to identify one that is rational, logical, objective, and consistent.

Our Worldview is an Interpretive Grid from Which We Form Answers

Some of us may not know we have a worldview. Still, whether conscious or subconscious, we all live according to some type of worldview. It's been forming for years and supports an assortment of everything we believe to be true. Ultimately, those beliefs are the stimulus behind our emotions, decisions, and actions. Our worldview includes an ideology, philosophy, movement, or system of belief that takes us down a path of awareness about God and the world. It affects our responses to the world, ourselves, and every other area of our life. It's our foundation for living.

Our worldview is an interpretive grid from which we form answers. Exploring and evaluating questions such as, "What is the nature of reality?", "Who or what am I?", "What is good for me?", "How do I know?" and "Can we test it?" helps us identify our worldview. And yes, we can test it. The diagrams below give two different worldview frames of reference:

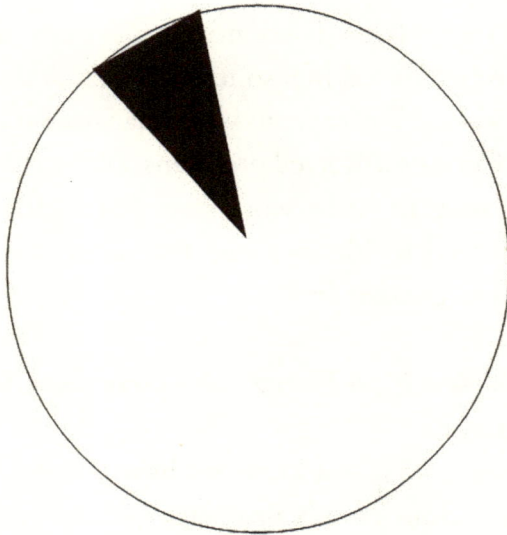

I choose to frame my worldview minimally through God's light and I live in darkness most of the time

Or

I choose to frame my worldview totally through God's light
and I live in his light all the time

We see the divergence of two worldview perspectives
between a most of the time frame of reference or an all the
time frame of reference. Two choices loom in our minds.
Do we want to live with a patchwork of incompatible
beliefs? Or do we want to live with an active, knowing,
interpretative grid that has been tested and deemed a true
and solid view of reality?

In a Difficult Situation, Some People May Choose to Disregard Their Worldview

We must live in this world, as it is now, rather than living a reclusive life in our own community. We need to be out there, in the world, rubbing elbows with every kind of person, even those with differing worldviews, and even those unaware of their worldview. Seeing the world as it really is, corrupt, evil, sinful and broken, prompts us to answer one or the other of two questions. What can we do to change it or how can we escape its brokenness?

Our response to these questions prompt us to either take action or walk away. Regardless, every action or lack thereof may come from family traditions, habits, and/or political ideologies. Our inborn desire is to do good in the world. Accordingly, when we make choices about how to respond to the world as it is (broken), some of us reflect on our worldview and try to apply God's patience, love, grace, and mercy to love the world and live beautifully despite its shortcomings. This usually requires a concentrated effort.

According to Stanley J. Grenz, in his book A Primer on Postmodernism, philosopher Immanuel Kant believed, "The mind is *active* in the knowing process" and that "the knowing process is fundamentally a relationship between the autonomous knowing self and the world waiting to be known through the creative power of the active mind." Accordingly, our mind dictates our picture of reality. We can't really see anything without a point of view. So, we guard against apathy, and work to develop an extensive, global view of reality, and see the world through our own filters of reality, which is our worldview.

For example, two people can evaluate a famine in South Sudan from entirely different worldviews. In one person's mind, the problem can't be solved because the South Sudanese government is corrupt. Sending food to the starving people is useless because it won't reach those in need. This person may feel a smidgeon of sympathy, but their view of reality doesn't include seeing themselves as a person suffering in Sudan. In the other person's mind, the problem is difficult to solve, because of systematic corruption in the country, but they continue to send food and pray for God's intervention. They feel empathy for children dying of hunger and believe that saving just one child is worth it. Please don't misunderstand. I'm not suggesting that all people must share the former or latter response. I'm simply showing how our worldviews differ. Furthermore, some people may choose not to explore, recognize, or speak of their worldview.

A Christ-Centered Worldview Causes Us to Examine Several Points

Since people differ from one another in their level of worldview thinking, a Christ-centered worldview requires that we look at four different levels of an individual's faith.

If a person has not yet converted to the Christian faith, we can't expect them to embrace a Christ-centered worldview.

If a person has converted to the Christian faith but is still aligned with secular, postmodern, or humanistic values, we can't yet expect them to fully embrace a Christ-centered worldview.

If a person has recently committed to authentic faith in God, it may take some time for them to grow into their Christ-centered worldview.

If a person was at one time a follower of Jesus and began to "backslide," it's never too late for them to return to Jesus.

Please note that in the above explanations, there is no finality in any one person's commitment to God, or worldview. We are all capable of changing our views at any time. Therefore, our prayer is that the first person will someday convert to Christianity, the second will eventually surrender to Christ, the third will mature into a Christ-centered worldview, and the fourth person will repent and come back to Jesus.

In 1 Peter 1:14, we read, "As obedient children, do not conform to the evil desires you had *when you lived in ignorance*" (emphasis added). Then in 1 Corinthians 13:7, Paul tells us, "Love bears all things, believes all things, hopes all things, endures all things" (ESV).

Accordingly, each of the above four persons deserve the benefit of the doubt, regarding their worldview.

Seven Big Picture Questions about Life

Defining a worldview as a personality is careless. Surely, we can do better than that. We can take the time to do our shopping, so to speak. Don't we want to evaluate competing worldviews and make an informed decision? The foundation of a true worldview encompasses man's belief (or unbelief) in a deity, as well as our origin and nature. Below are seven big-picture questions to help us discover our worldview:

Is there a God and what is he like?
What is the nature and origin of the universe?
What is the nature and origin of humankind?
What happens to people after they die?
Where does knowledge come from?
What is the basis of ethics and morality?
What is the meaning of human history?

Try to find the answers to these questions in the Bible. We want to prepare ourselves to recognize false or competing worldviews. Each worldview makes claims to truth. But in the case of Marxism, for example, you will find that their claim to the secret of life resides in economics, and that reality is found in the conflicts between those who control the means of production and those who don't. Clearly, our answers to the above questions would tell us that Marxism isn't a biblical worldview.

Making Sure Our Thinking is Compatible with Biblical Truth is Crucial

All of us operate from a worldview, even those who think they don't have one. The latter fail to recognize what a worldview really is, call it rose-colored glasses, a frame of reference, or simply judgments based on perception, all of these make up a worldview. How can we establish a Christ-centered worldview? There are challenges, but none are so formidable that they can't be overcome. We ask ourselves certain questions to evaluate our core beliefs. We want to ensure our thinking is compatible with biblical truth. If it isn't, we can abandon false ideas and look to the Bible to modify them. A recent George Barna survey offers eight questions that help us determine if our worldview is consistent with biblical teaching:

> Do absolute moral truths exist?
>
> Did Jesus Christ live a sinless life?
>
> Is God the all-powerful and all-knowing creator of the universe, and does he still rule it today?
>
> Is salvation a gift from God that cannot be earned?
>
> Is Satan real?
>
> Is the Bible accurate in all of its teachings?

Additionally, I would add, "Does a Christian have a responsibility to share their faith in Christ with other people?" and "Is absolute truth defined in the Bible?" The answers to these questions are valuable, but more importantly, they reveal if our life shows our commitment to a Christ-centered worldview. Yes, we are all sinners. We all fall short of the glory of God. Still, even as the sinners that we are, our responses to other people and the world will divulge our deepest, most honest, and valid beliefs about God's plans for redemption of the world.

When We Commit Ourselves to a Christ-Centered Worldview, Our Lives Spring Anew

The hope of redemption and restoration belongs only to the Christ-centered worldview. "Let us hold unswervingly to the *hope* we profess, for he who promised is faithful." (Hebrews 10:23, emphasis added). Biblical hope, translated from the Greek word "elpis", means "certain, an assurance for the future." Paul gives a summation of the completion of God's promises:

> *But when the kindness and love of God our Savior appeared, he saved us, not because of righteous things we had done, but because of his mercy. He saved us through the washing of rebirth and renewal by the Holy Spirit, whom he poured out on us generously through Jesus Christ our Savior, so that, having been justified by his grace, we might become heirs having the hope of eternal life* (Titus 3:4–7).

No other worldview offers such a welcoming expectation for the future, nor do they promise eternal life. So, what exactly is a Christ-centered worldview?

In *Worldview*, Christian worldview expert David Naugle wrote, "'Worldview' in a Christian perspective implies the objective existence of the Trinitarian God whose essential character establishes the moral order of the universe and whose word, wisdom, and law define and govern all aspects of created existence."

In other words, the Father, Son, and Holy Spirit, who created the universe, demonstrate and authenticate how we live in and relate to the world. This worldview, based on the flawless Word of God, requires productive thinking regarding the Christian faith. When we commit ourselves to a Christ-centered worldview, our lives spring anew while we study and contemplate the Bible, rejoicing at the revelation of God's plan.

In addition, when we believe that the Bible is truth without exception, we give our Christ- centered worldview permission to dictate everything we say and do. For example, we acknowledge Paul's admonitions found in Romans 13:

Be a good citizen. All governments are under God (Rom. 13:1, MSG).

The police aren't there just to be admired in their uniforms. God also has an interest in keeping order, and he uses them to do it (Rom. 13:4, MSG).

Pay your taxes, pay your bills, respect your leaders (Rom. 13:7, MSG).

Don't run up debts, except for the huge debt of love you owe each other . . . Love other people as well as you do yourself (Rom. 13:8–9, MSG).

You can't go wrong when you love others. When you add up everything in the law code, the sum total is love (Rom. 13:10, MSG).

Be up and awake to what God is doing! God is putting the finishing touches on the salvation work he began when we first believed. We can't afford to waste a minute (Rom. 13:12–13, MSG).

Don't loiter and linger, waiting until the very last minute (Rom. 13:14, MSG).

Dress yourselves in Christ, and be up and about (Rom. 13:14, MSG).

A Christ-centered worldview is a conscious and subconscious proposition from which we learn to live beautifully in a broken world.

What We Do Today Has an Effect on Tomorrow

You may be saying, "Okay that's well and good, but I'm not really sure I can commit myself to Christianity or the Christ-centered worldview." This is an understandable comment, because many of us want to live freely without obligations. Some people may feel like they are good people and therefore see no need for Christ. Further, because we claim God is good, they might question, "If God is so good, then why would he want to send me, a good person, to hell?" God doesn't want to send anybody to hell. But as discussed in Chapter seven, destruction is our destiny without salvation brought to fruition by Christ.

We can also see from history that what we do today has an effect on tomorrow. Therefore, we look back at creation and the fall (where our sin began). We look now at the cross and Christ's redemptive act (where our sin is forgiven). Finally, we look forward to

Time Out

What does being good citizen mean? Can't I protest? Of course, you can protest. Being a good citizen means when you do protest, do it peacefully and for a reason that's less about self-interest and more about the good of humanity, based on God's purposes for the world. In addition to Paul's explanation, a good citizen resists apathy, indifference, and a lack of caring for what's going on in the world. We don't have to protest as much as we need to pray daily for our country and the world.

the second coming of Christ, and the New Jerusalem (an eternity without the effects of sin). Paul wrote, "I consider that our present sufferings are not worth comparing with the glory that will be revealed in us" (Rom. 8:18). Revelation also reveals:

> *"He will wipe every tear from their eyes. There will be no more death' or mourning or crying or pain, for the old order of things has passed away"* (Rev. 21:4).

Although God will create the new heavens and the new earth, those of us with a Christ- centered worldview respond by telling the world the Good News, and inspiring others to seek absolute truth, who is God. Only through this type of action can we Christians with Christ- centered worldviews help resolve the problem of sin. Carl Henry (1913-2003), an American Evangelical Christian theologian, wrote, "Man's destiny is therefore not simply an endless existence, but is moral—either a life redeemed and fit for eternity, or a life under perpetual divine judgment." By putting into practice those ultimate and perfect revelations found in God's Word, we are fit to dwell in eternity with Him.

How Much More Do We Need?

It's never too late to establish a worldview that's compatible with deity, origin, and nature. We can always begin by picking up a Bible. The life lessons throughout the Bible are as applicable now as they were in the times of Moses, Abraham, David, Isaiah, Solomon, Jesus, Matthew, Mark, Luke, John, and Paul. The disciples teach us in the different ways that Jesus shared with them. In 2 Peter 1:3– 9 we are encouraged to confirm our election and calling, when we read:

> *His divine power has given us everything we need for a godly life through our knowledge of him who called us by his own glory and goodness. Through these he has given us his very great and precious promises, so that through them you may participate in the divine nature, having escaped the corruption in the world caused by evil desires. For this very reason, make every effort to add to your faith goodness; and to goodness, knowledge; and to knowledge, self-control; and to self-control, perseverance; and to perseverance, godliness; and to godliness, mutual affection; and to mutual affection, love. For if you possess these qualities in increasing measure, they will keep you from being ineffective and unproductive in your knowledge of our Lord Jesus Christ. But whoever does not have them is nearsighted and blind, forgetting that they have been cleansed from their past sins* (2 Peter 1:3–9).

Through Jesus' divine power and nature, we can live a godly life by adding the qualities of Jesus to our faith. How much more do we need? The most beautiful aspect of a life centered on Christ and a Christ-centered worldview is that once we've invited Jesus into our lives, he is never taken away nor will he leave us.

I can't imagine not having Christ as the focus in my life. Surrendering to him made me a different person. During the best and worst of times, Jesus is always there for me. He gives me the freedom and confidence to live within his purposes for my life, because he surrounds me with his teachings, his patience, his love, mercy, and grace. What more do I need? More important, what more do any of us need?

Reflection Questions

1. What was your worldview before reading this book?

2. How do you think an ordinary person can change the world?

3. How do you feel about giving others the "benefit of the doubt"?

4. What are your thoughts about the seven questions that determine if your beliefs are compatible with biblical teaching?

5. How would you describe the notion that what we do today has an effect on tomorrow?

CHAPTER ELEVEN

Final Thoughts

The world is a book, and those who do not travel read only a page. Faith is to believe what you do not yet see; the reward for this faith is to see what you believe. Since love grows within you, so beauty grows. For love is the beauty of the soul.

– Saint Augustine of Hippo

HERE WE ARE, at the conclusion of my labor, written out of love for others. Like birthing a newborn, a bit of sadness overwhelms me in the midst of great joy. I've been carrying this precious book inside me for so long. I know I will miss it. The pains of writing it, the "aha" moments, and the life-changing observations I've learned about you and me will always remain close to my heart.

Traveling down this path of research, reading, studying, and writing has been both a joy and a struggle. My prayer is that you felt encouraged, informed, and loved by what you read. My intentions were to focus primarily on making us aware of the pitfalls that surround us and encouraging us to love the world as God does, while mourning its brokenness. This paradoxical love relationship with the world is the epitome of living beautifully in a broken world.

If the chapters in this book caused you to think differently or to seek a new path for your life, good for you! Not that your former path was so bad, but that your new path gives you the assurance of God's sacrificial love for you and all the blessings that come from your sacred romance with him.

Can you love him more than yourself? Can you surrender yourself to his care and comfort? A love affair with the living God is the best of the best that life has to offer. As the lover of our souls, God takes us as we are, rebellious, rowdy, and rude. We deserve absolutely nothing from him. And yet, he loves beyond what we can imagine and he never stops. Until the last day, Jesus will continue to invite us:

> *"Come to me, all you who are weary and burdened, and I will give you rest. Take my yoke upon you and learn from me, for I am gentle and humble in heart, and you will find rest for your souls. For my yoke is easy and my burden is light"* (Matt. 11:28–30).

If you've not made a decision for Christ, he will wait. Jesus tells us:

"What do you think? If a man owns a hundred sheep, and one of them wanders away, will he not leave the ninety-nine on the hills and go to look for the one that wandered off? And if he finds it, truly I tell you, he is happier about that one sheep than about the ninety-nine that did not wander off. In the same way your Father in heaven is not willing that any of these little ones should perish (Matt. 18:12–14).

Even when we've run far from Jesus, his patience, love, mercy, and grace abound. Still, Jesus prunes us, so that we will bear fruit.

"I am the true vine, and my Father is the gardener. He cuts off every branch in me that bears no fruit, while every branch that does bear fruit he prunes so that it will be even more fruitful. You are already clean because of the word I have spoken to you. Remain in me, as I also remain in you. No branch can bear fruit by itself; it must remain in the vine. Neither can you bear fruit unless you remain in me. I am the vine; you are the branches. If you remain in me and I in you, you will bear much fruit; apart from me you can do nothing. If you do not remain in me, you are like a branch that is thrown away and withers; such branches are picked up, thrown into the fire and burned. If

you remain in me and my words remain in you,
ask whatever you wish, and it will be done for you"
(John 15:1–7).

Turning the last pages of this book is like closing the door on one of my dreams. On the other hand, there is nothing as sweet as opening the door on a new dream except for Christ living within me. My next dream, and there will be a next dream, will present itself according to God's purposes and excellent timing. Until then, and at this moment, I ask for your permission to pray for you and for me.

Dear Father God, precious Jesus, and Holy Spirit,

Please be gathered here with us as we praise you and thank you for all of your creation. I pray, Lord, that we would never lose sight of your universe and all of its adornments, fashioned by you, and made to give us pleasure and sustenance. Help us, Father, to view the world in which we live as you do: with patience, love, mercy, and grace. Forgive us for making snap judgements about other people's identities, knowing that until we spend time in conversation, we aren't really aware of what they think, how they live, and what their beliefs are. Give us wisdom, dear God, to look at the realities of the world with sound and reasoned points of view.

Precious Father, may we always find the utmost of pleasure as beings created by you with unconditional love, all body parts perfectly in sync, and made for your purposes. At the same time, Lord, help us to discern what those purposes are, from season to season, in all circumstances, so that we may be pleasing in your sight. Make us aware of our inner thoughts, our shortcomings, and our lack of understanding of those around us. Please direct our hearts and minds to your Word, so that we may grasp the significance of your promises and look to them with full assurance for our lives now and in the future.

We acknowledge that we're sick with sin, but find healing through your solution to our problem. We rejoice in your Son's perfect life here on earth, and solemnly remember his sacrifice, taking our sins upon his shoulders, hated and reviled by humanity. May we never take these things for granted. Please, Lord, help us to remember that only through Christ's resurrection from the dead can we also have eternal life.

Give us your wisdom, Father, to avail ourselves of the resources you've provided so that we may understand the historical facts surrounding the birth, ministry, death, and resurrection of Jesus Christ. Help us, dear God, to search, find, study, understand, surrender, and commit ourselves to the Lord, Jesus Christ. Guide us away from cultural viewpoints that deny you as God. Lead us into authentic faith that draws us nearer to you. Give us the courage to reject superficial spirituality and self-love that we may embrace with reverence the reality of who you are and what you've done for us.

Father God, we ask that you teach us how to live beautifully in this broken world. To love all of humanity unconditionally as you do. Help us to see this world through your unblemished eyesight, so that we see your original plans for each person we encounter. Thank you for your abundant blessings in our lives. We pray all of these things in the sweet and precious name of Jesus Christ.

Amen.

Acknowledgments

SOMEONE ONCE TOLD me "writing a book is one of the hardest things to do." That is so true. Which is why I want to express my heartfelt gratitude to the many people who encouraged, supported, and kept me on track for the past two years.

First, I want to thank God for giving me the desire to write. I couldn't have finished it without his presence in my life. Mike Klassen, my writing coach, spent endless hours making what I wanted to say better. His ability to understand what I was trying to say, and pointing out when my words didn't make sense was invaluable. His patience, knowledge, optimism, and inspiration kept me going when I was ready to throw in the towel. I couldn't have done it without you, Mike.

Thanks to my writing cohorts who showed me love, respect, and honest feedback of my work, Judith Rose and Annee McHughes. My second cousin, Velda, offered me the opportunity to speak and share about my book at a women's conference at her church. Thanks, Velda.

And to my daughter, Robin, I so appreciate your interest in the project and your priceless abilities that will bring the book to market in extraordinary ways that only you would think of. I really appreciate it, sweetie.

Many thanks to Rob Campbell, the head shot photographer who dusted me off and made me shine.

To those who read the manuscript either one chapter at a time or when finished: Alberta Kontio, Denise Morris, Dan Gardinier, Jeff Lynch, Stephen Bossom, Butch Pritchett, and Joyce Breheny endless thanks for taking your valuable time to read my work. Katie Sherbondy, you certainly had your work cut out for you when you took on the job of copyediting. Thanks, your attention to detail was invaluable.

My family and friends deserve a round of thanks for being patient with me when my mind was on the manuscript and should've been somewhere else, and when I turned down invitations because I had to "keep going on my manuscript."

Most of all, I want to thank my wonderful and supportive husband, Scott, who didn't complain when I spent hours in front of the computer instead of with him. He cooked meals, cleaned the house, and was patient with my moodiness when my writing had taken a wrong turn. Thanks honey. Love you always.

Sources

Ashbrook, R. Thomas. *Mansions of the Heart: Exploring the Seven Stages of Spiritual Growth*. San Francisco: Jossey-Bass, 2009.

Bonhoeffer, Dietrich. *Letters and Papers from Prison,* New York: Touchstone, 1997.

Brand, Paul and Philip Yancey. *Fearfully and Wonderfully Made*. Grand Rapids: Zondervan, 1980.

Carter, Stephen L. *The Culture of Disbelief: How American Law and Politics Trivialize Religious Devotion*. New York: Anchor Books, 1993.

Chambers, Oswald. *My Utmost For His Highest: Daily Devotional Journal*. Uhrichsville, OH: Barbour Publishing, 1963.

Coskun, Orhan and Darin Butler. "Turkey vows to cleanse Islamic State from border after wedding attack." *World News*, August 20, 2016. Accessed September 2, 2017. http://www.reuters.com/article/us-turkey-blast/turkey-vows-to-cleanse-islamic-state-from-border-after-wedding-attack-idUSKCN10V0TG.

Curtis, Brent and John Eldredge. *The Sacred Romance: Drawing Closer to the Heart of God*. Nashville: Thomas Nelson, 1997.

Dark, David. *Life's Too Short to Pretend You're Not Religious*. Downers Grove, IL: InterVarsity Press, 2016.

DiBlasio, Natalie. "Mother charged with burning newborn to death." *USA Today*, January 17, 2015. Accessed September 2, 2017. https://www.usatoday.com/story/news/nation/2015/01/17/newborn-dies-fire-new-jersey/21919481/.

Foster, Richard J. *Celebration of Discipline: The Path to Spiritual Growth, 25th Anniversary Edition*. San Francisco: Harper Collins, 1998.

González, Justo L. *The Story of Christianity: Volume II: The Reformation to the Present Day*. New York: Harper Collins, 2010.

Grenz, Stanley J. *A Primer on Postmodernism*. Grand Rapids: Wm. B. Eerdmans Publishing Co., 1996.

Grudem, Wayne. *Systematic Theology: An Introduction to Biblical Doctrine*. Grand Rapids: Zondervan, 1994.

Gundry, Robert H. *A Survey of the New Testament: 4th Ed.* Grand Rapids: Zondervan, 2003.

Keller, Timothy, *The Meaning of Marriage: The Complexities of Commitment with the Wisdom of God*. Grand Rapids: Zondervan, 2015.

Lewis, C. S. *Mere Christianity*. New York: Touchstone, 1996.

MacArthur, John. *Twelve Extraordinary Women: How God Shaped Women of the Bible and What He Wants to do With You.* Nashville: Thomas Nelson, 2005.

Moore, Beth. *Breaking Free: Making Liberty in Christ a Reality in Life*. Nashville: Broadman & Holman Publishers, 1999.

Naugle, David K. *Worldview: The History of a Concept.* Grand Rapids: Eerdmans, 2002.

Parkinson, Joe and David George-Cosh. "Image of Drowned Syrian Boy Echoes Around World." *The Wall Street Journal*, September 3, 2015. Accessed September 2, 2017. https://www.wsj.com/articles/image-of-syrian-boy-washed-up-on-beach-hits-hard-1441282847.

Phillips, Noelle. "Four Denver women held captive, assaulted in garage beating." *The Denver Post*, August 19, 2015. Accessed September 2, 2017. http://www.denverpost.com/2015/08/19/four-denver-women-held-captive-assaulted-in-garage-beating/.

Phillips, W. Gary, William E. Brown, and John Stonestreet. *Making Sense of Your World: A Biblical Worldview 2nd Ed.* Salem, WI: Sheffield Publishing Company, 2008.

Schaeffer, Edith. *Christianity is Jewish*. Wheaton: Tyndale, 1975.

Smith, Gordon T. *Courage and Calling: Embracing Your God-Given Potential.* Downers Grove, IL: InterVarsity Press, 1999.

Strassner, Kurt. *Opening Up Genesis.* Leominster, England: Day One Publications, 2009. Logos Research Systems.

Tozer, A. W. *The Pursuit of God: The Human Thirst for the Divine.* Camp Hill, PA: Wing Spread Publishers, 2006.

Wallis, Jim. *God's Politics: Why the Right Gets it Wrong and the Left Doesn't Get It: A New Vision for Faith and Politics in America.* New York: Harper Collins, 2005.

Willmington, H. L. *The Complete Book of Bible Lists.* Wheaton: Tyndale House, 1987.

Author Biography

CAROL FLOHR GILES is an author, blogger, and speaker, who offers a biblical perspective on the joy and challenge of Christian living in a non-Christian world. After raising her family and retiring from the retail business she ran with her husband for twenty years, she earned a bachelor's degree in Biblical Studies from Colorado Christian University at the age of seventy. An active leader in her church, Carol has taught numerous classes and Bible studies, led international mission trips, and has shared her testimony with congregations in multiple countries.

In *Calming the Chaos: How to Live Beautifully in a Broken World*, she uses a fresh, yet realistic voice to help readers apply biblical truths to their everyday lives. Her first book, *Call of the Potter* (available on Amazon), narrates the many struggles, setbacks, and triumphs of her journey from a dysfunctional childhood to becoming whole as a devoted follower of Christ. She is currently working on a Bible study with accompanying workbook based on the lessons of *Calming the Chaos: How to Live Beautifully in a Broken World*.

You can reach Carol through her web site www.carolflohrgiles.com.